fP

To Harvey Rubenstein,

with best regards,

from

[signature]

THE FREE PRESS
New York London Toronto Sydney Singapore

FAITH

or

FEAR

How Jews Can Survive
in a Christian America

ELLIOTT ABRAMS

THE FREE PRESS
A Division of Simon & Schuster Inc.
1230 Avenue of the Americas
New York, NY 10020

Designed by Carla Bolte

Manufactured in the United States of America

10 9 8 7 6 5 4 3 2

Library of Congress Cataloging-in-Publication Data

Abrams, Elliott.
    Faith or fear: how Jews can survive in a Christian America /
Elliott Abrams.
      p. cm.
    Includes bibliographical references and index.
    1. Judaism—United States. 2. Jews—Cultural assimilation—
United States. 3. Judaism—United States—Relations—Chris-
tianity. 4. Christianity and other religions—Judaism.   I. Title.

  BM205.A28   1997
  296′.0973′09045—dc21   97–4966
                                    CIP

ISBN 0–684–82511–2

FOR MY CHILDREN,
JACOB, SARAH, AND JOSEPH

CONTENTS

PREFACE

WHENEVER I speak or write about religious affairs or about the Jewish community, I am asked how I came to this subject matter and what my own religious practices are. While the ideas presented here must stand and fall on their own, it is still a fair question.

I grew up in intimate contact with Yiddish-speaking maternal grandparents who had arrived from Galicia, now part of Ukraine, and lived on New York's Lower East Side and then in the Bronx. They read English slowly and with the greatest difficulty. They and literally everyone I knew in their generation spoke English with strong Yiddish accents (in fact, as a child I believed that when I was old I would, like them, have gray hair, walk slowly, and speak with an accent). Their life in America, like that of most immigrant Jews of their generation, was a success: they became citizens, sent their children to college, and owned a row house and a small tailor shop. They would have added that all their children married Jews, and kept kosher homes.

They lived in New York City surrounded by immigrants from dozens of other countries, but their world was divided into two groups: Jews, and everyone else—non-Jews whose private lives never mixed with theirs. They had come to America and become

Americans, but like millions of immigrants from other places, much of American society was alien to them. They had immigrated; integration was for their children; assimilation was inconceivable. For above all, they lived their lives as Jews, and that fact conditioned everything that happened to them, what they thought, and what they did.

The transitional generation was that of my parents, both born around the time of World War I, when the great waves of Jewish immigration to America were ending. They were raised in Jewish neighborhoods in New York City, spoke Yiddish before they spoke English, and grew up living among the immigrants. The brightest dividing line for them and for very many Jews of their generation was still between "them" and "us"—between Christians and Jews. But they were Americans, spoke unaccented English, were college graduates, and raised my brother and me in a suburban environment worlds away from the Lower East Side. Yiddish was disappearing, children went away to college, gentiles were neighbors, and most Jews were becoming less and less Jewish. Their generation knew perfectly well what it meant to be a Jew and wanted to discover instead the possibilities inherent in being an American.

My generation is fully integrated into American society, and the question it faces is whether to remain Jewish in any meaningful sense. I write as a practicing Jew who is raising his children as Jews. I can probably best be described as a somewhat observant Conservative Jew, and I do not argue here for Orthodoxy of any variety, religious or political. Like most non-Orthodox American Jews who try to take their religion seriously, I find my own religious education inadequate and must deal with that shortcoming now, as an adult. Like most who are parents, I find raising children a never-ending balancing act. My wife and I want our children to identify as Jews, marry Jews, and raise their own children as Jews, but at the same time we want them to move freely in this open society. We try to convey to them the faith that we share, and in this at least we feel no uncertainty. We teach them what we believe: that the covenant of Abraham abides today and that they have been blessed to be born into it.

I have dedicated this book to my children. Reversing the sad demographic trends of recent decades will require the efforts of their generation. Similarly, the marginalization of religion in America has taken decades, and will require much work to reverse. If there is success, it will come in their time.

ACKNOWLEDGMENTS

THIS BOOK was undertaken with the encouragement of my former colleagues at the Hudson Institute, where I worked from 1990 until 1996, and with constant help from Hudson's superb library staff.

I wish to thank my agent, Glen Hartley, for his consistently thoughtful advice on how to turn a set of ideas into a book. I am deeply grateful to the Carthage Foundation for its very generous support for this project.

Those who were kind enough to read early drafts of the manuscript—Norman Podhoretz, Father Richard Neuhaus, and especially the incomparable Midge Decter—offered me wise counsel, although neither they nor anyone else except the author bears responsibility for any errors found here.

I owe a special debt to my wife, Rachel, who was, as always, my first reader and my best critic.

Chapter 1

CRISIS

S INCE THE earliest decades of this century, the American Jewish community has seemed the safest and most successful of them all. It was not, until the Nazis, larger than the Jewish communities of Europe, nor did it provide Judaism's most revered scholars. But at least since World War I, its growing size, wealth, and political influence have given it special prestige and self-confidence.

Until now. The results of the National Jewish Population Study of 1990, and several other major works of research, draw the portrait of a community in decline, facing in fact a demographic disaster. The term "disaster" is no exaggeration:

- Jews, who once comprised 3.7 percent of the U.S. population, have fallen to about 2 percent.
- One-third of all Americans of Jewish ancestry no longer report Judaism as their religion.
- Of all Jews who have married since 1985, the majority have married non-Jews, while the rate of conversion of non-Jewish spouses is declining.
- Only 28 percent of the children of intermarried couples are raised as Jews.

1

- Demographers predict a drop of anywhere from one million to over two million in the American Jewish population in the next two generations.

The Vanishing American Jew?

The demographic disaster facing American Jewry has come as a shock to most Jews, who long believed that their community was flourishing.

Although Orthodox authorities in nineteenth- and early-twentieth-century eastern Europe sometimes argued that Judaism could not thrive in America, such voices were rare. And the data seemed to support the view that assimilation was a small danger. Jews had the lowest intermarriage rate of any group in New York City in data collected in 1870, 1900, 1930, and 1940. Even in 1959, the *American Jewish Year Book* reported that the rate was only 7.2 percent. In fact in all the *Year Books* published from 1900 to 1963, intermarriage was dealt with only once, and then in two brief pages.[1] In their seminal book, *Beyond the Melting Pot,* Daniel P. Moynihan and Nathan Glazer noted that even in the 1960s, Jews continued to marry Jews.

Moreover, there had seemed to be an upsurge of Jewish community affiliation in the years after World War II. As Jews moved to the suburbs, they did not try to leave the Jewish community. On the contrary, they built new synagogues, most often Conservative synagogues, and sent their children there for Hebrew school.

And other events appeared to bear witness to the greater strength and cohesiveness of the American Jewish community. There had been a long debate over Zionism, pitting members of the Reform movement and other Jewish elites in this country who opposed the idea of Jewish nationalism against what was probably the majority of eastern European Jews. But with the founding of the state of

Israel in 1948, the debate ended. American Jews became dedicated supporters of Israel, and that support rose to new heights of enthusiasm after the 1967 War. Israel was a cause that rallied all but a few fringe elements in the community, including many whose religious commitments had lapsed.

The organizations that specialized in raising money for Israel, and indeed those that served the entire community, raised ever-higher amounts of money with each passing year. Jewish philanthropy, with its hospitals, old-age homes, defense against anti-Semitism, and sustenance for Israel, seemed to be the heart of Jewish community life—and to be beating strongly.

In the 1970s and 1980s the plight of Jews in the Soviet Union gave rise to widespread activism in the community as well. Local and national organizations provided aid to Jewish brethren living under oppression and pressed the U.S. government to push the Soviets harder to let them emigrate. "Refuseniks" like Anatoly Scharansky became Jewish heroes in the United States.

And those decades saw a great increase in interest in the Holocaust. The 1940s and 1950s, a time when the Holocaust was so much closer, had seen no such phenomenon, and the impact of the Holocaust on American Jews was hard to measure. The effect on American Christians seemed clearer, for in the aftermath of the Holocaust, anti-Semitism in America—and especially the public expression of that anti-Semitism—lost its social acceptability. For American Jews, the fate of Europe's Jews certainly cemented support for the state of Israel and ended the long debate over Zionism. But the Holocaust itself did not dominate the discourse of the Jewish community, and discussions of its historical roots, religious meaning, or detailed chronology were far from the center of American Jewish life.

But by the 1980s, the event was studied intensely, and American Jews were much better informed about it than they had ever been before. College courses multiplied, scores of books were published and were widely read in the Jewish community, the new Holocaust Memorial Museum in Washington, D.C., and several others around the country were built, and the subject became a central focus of Jewish attention.

From many points of view, then, the American Jewish community seemed lively and strong. Its institutions were well funded and active, and several causes won the enthusiastic backing of its members. America's Jews were integrating into the society at large—in residential, educational, and employment patterns—but did not seem to be assimilating. How could there be a crisis developing here?

But as it happens, the underlying trends began to change as early as the 1960s. The American Jewish community was less and less Jewish, more and more assimilated. Jews began to study, work, and live among Christians. The "restricted" neighborhood became extremely rare, few jobs (including that of senator or governor) and no campuses were off-limits to Jews, and they became fully integrated into American economic, social, and political life. With that integration and the continuing decline in anti-Semitism, Jews and Christians began to marry each other as well, in ever-increasing numbers.

Under the trappings of success, erosion began. Marshall Sklare, the great sociologist of American Jewry at Brandeis University, was among the first to notice. In April 1964 he expressed worry about what the rising intermarriage figures meant, and called intermarriage a "bitter dilemma" that "casts into doubt American Jewry's dual ideal of full participation in the society and the preservation of Jewish identity."[2]

The following month, *Look* magazine published its famous article entitled "The Vanishing American Jew," which argued that the Jewish community was diminishing in size.[3] It was easy to mock the article as a gross overstatement of the evidence, and it did not *seem* that Jews were vanishing. But by 1970, the National Jewish Population Study showed that the previously very low levels of intermarriage had begun to rise—from 8 percent in the 1940s and 10 percent for 1960–64, to 23 percent for 1965–71. Some scholars began to question whether the Jewish community was in truth as healthy as it seemed.

Sklare's warning had come in 1964. In 1973 Charles Liebman, now professor of political studies at Bar Ilan University, read the data and saw what was coming. Liebman recalled Will Herberg's description of America as a land of three religions: Protestant-Catholic-Jew. "The Jew today," Liebman wrote, "at the level of popular culture and belief, is not thought of as constituting 2.6 or even 3 percent of American society. The Jew is one-third of America." But the so-called Judeo-Christian ethic was better yet: "we can go even further and give the Jew one-half share in the Judeo-Christian heritage upon which our secular society is presumably based." The problem was that these notions were increasingly at odds with reality, and Liebman asked, "at what point does American society and its political, cultural, and economic institutions become conscious of the fact" that Jewish status far outweighs Jewish numbers?[4]

Statistics showed that only 49 percent of Jews who married between 1975 and 1984 married other Jews, while the number of non-Jewish spouses converting to Judaism was steadily declining.[5] Still, the worries shared by Sklare and Liebman were dismissed by others. In 1985, Charles Silberman, a journalist, produced a Jewish best-seller entitled *A Certain People* in which he took a resolutely optimistic view of American Jewry. "We are," he said, "in fact, in the early stages of a major revitalization of Jewish religious, intellectual, and cultural life—one that is likely to transform as well as strengthen American Judaism."[6] He was not unduly concerned about rising intermarriage rates, for "it seems unlikely that intermarriage will lead to more than a slight reduction in the number of Jews, and it could bring about an increase."[7] He reasoned that if the children of intermarried couples were raised as Jews, these marriages would provide new recruits to the Jewish population. Anyway, "there is reason to believe that the increase has about run its course and that it may stabilize at the current level. It is even possible that intermarriage may decline somewhat over the next decade or two."[8]

Silberman was far from alone. Calvin Goldscheider, professor of Judaic studies and sociology at Brown University, concurred in his 1986 book *Jewish Continuity and Change*. "There is every evidence of Jewish continuity in America in a transformed community," he wrote.[9] He understood that Jews were less and less attached to their religion, but "the decline in the centrality of religion must be seen in the context of the emergence of new forms of Jewish expression." There were other ways to be Jewish, even if the "links between religion and Jewishness have weakened. These new forms provide a wide range of options for expressing Jewishness . . . for most, Jewishness is a combination of family, communal, religious, and ethnic forms of Jewish expression."[10] That the community was less religious and more secular did not seem to him to suggest trouble.

"The secularization of Judaism and Jews has long been observed in America," Goldscheider reminded readers. "The critical question is whether alternative sources of group cohesion have emerged as religious centrality has declined."[11] And he thought that new forms of Jewishness as powerful as the old bond of Judaism per se had indeed developed.

Nor was he troubled by intermarriage rates. For one thing, they did not necessarily imply that the Jewish community would decline in size: "The limited evidence suggests that there are no simple connections between increases in intermarriage levels and demographic erosion of the American-Jewish community."[12]

There were plenty of data to toss around in the 1980s, and it was still possible for observers of talent and intelligence to take different sides. Trends might be overinterpreted, or slow down, or even reverse themselves. The Jewish community was not, after all, an object in a laboratory, bound by the laws of physics. It might change, react, evolve, and it certainly has. To a degree even pessimists did not anticipate, those "alternative sources of group cohesion" and "new forms of Jewish expression" based in "Jewishness" rather than Judaism have failed; intermarriage rates are rising; and the Jewish population is falling.

Demographic Disaster

The truth about the condition of the American Jewish community emerged from the 1990 National Jewish Population Study. "The new data show the substantive debate is over. To our deep regret, the pessimists, or rather the realists, were proven to be right," wrote the Israeli demographer Sergio della Pergola for the American Jewish Congress in 1992.[13] Paul Ritterband of the Center for Jewish Studies of the City University of New York was even more blunt.

> The 1990 National Jewish Population Survey has put an end to some key illusions. American exceptionalism does not exist. American Jewry is going the way of other emancipated diaspora Jewish communities. Intermarriage rates are high, fertility is low. While the end is not in sight, we are living on the edge of the steep slope of dissolution. Claims to the contrary notwithstanding, American Jews are not being transformed, they are being assimilated.[14]

In the late 1980s, demographers reported that there were 5.7 million Jews in America in 1985, and they predicted a drop to 5.4 million in 2000 and to 4.7 million by 2020.[15] More recently the sociologists Seymour Martin Lipset and Earl Raab of Brandeis University warned that the Jewish community would be reduced to a "hard core minimum" of one-half its present size in two generations, or about 40 years.[16] This would be a loss not of one but more than two million. Jews have long had a fertility rate about one-third lower than other Americans, and given the American rate right now, a report for the American Jewish Congress was correct in saying that "Jews are past ZPG [zero population growth]."[17] One contributing factor is the later age at marriage: A 1985 survey of the Boston area Jewish population found that just under a quarter of all Jews between the ages of thirty and thirty-nine had never been married.[18] The post-World War II generation of Jewish families with mom, dad, and two children is being replaced: far more Jews than ever before never marry, marry late, have one or no children, or marry non-Jews and do not raise their children as Jews.

Thus Jews, once 3.7 percent of the American population, are now only about 2 percent.[19] Among the many ramifications of a smaller population is that it is harder for young Jews to find Jewish spouses. Delayed marriage means as well that instead of seeking a spouse at a university whose student population may be one-fourth or one-third Jewish, young Jewish men and women now seek spouses later in the broader society, where Jews are much scarcer.

Jews once lived in dense and vibrant settlements. Today they are spread all across America, having joined the move to the Sunbelt. In their 1993 book about religion in America, *One Nation Under God,* Barry Kosmin and Seymour P. Lachman of the City University of New York reported that

Jewish population distribution is now much closer to the U.S. population as a whole than it was even forty years ago. Forty percent of

8

America's Jews by religion now live in the southern and western regions of the country (the figure was only 12% in 1930). . . . Jews are much more mobile than any other religious group of the country.[20]

All the data suggest that as Jewish population density and the age of the community decline, everything from synagogue affiliation to in-marriage declines with it.[21] As a result, population distribution, a matter of mild interest for other religious groups, becomes yet another harbinger of trouble for the Jews. Synagogue affiliation is much lower in the South and West than in the North and East, yet Jews are moving to precisely those low-membership regions.[22] Intermarriage data are similar: Jews aged eighteen to twenty-nine in Philadelphia had an intermarriage rate of 38 percent in the 1980s, but the rate was 72 percent in Denver and in Phoenix.[23]

How many Jews are left in America today? Only twenty-five years ago it would have been easy to answer the question, but today it is not. *The American Jewish Year Book,* which is published by the American Jewish Committee, offers guidance.[24]

- 3.2 million households contain one or more Jews or former Jews, and those households contain 8.2 million people.
- 6.8 million of them are Jews or are people of Jewish descent.
- But of those 6.8 million, 1.1 million were secular Jews, saying they now had no religion.
- And another 1.3 million were people of Jewish descent now professing another religion.

(Of that 1.3 million, 415,000 were adults raised from birth in another religion and were usually children of mixed marriages; 700,000 were children under eighteen with one Jewish parent and being raised in another religion; 210,000 were born or raised Jewish and now professing another religion.) *Roughly 12 percent of Americans of Jewish heritage are now Christians.*

Subtracting the 1.3 million people now belonging to other religions from the 6.8 million who are Jews or of Jewish descent, we can define what is called the "core" Jewish population of 5.5 million. But of that "core" itself, 1.1 million say they now have no religion and consider themselves secular Jews. *That is, 20 percent of the "core" Jewish population has left the Jewish religion.* Considering how unlikely it is that their children will be raised as Jews and will marry Jews, we can see why the prognosis is grim. There may be 6.8 million people of Jewish descent or converted into Judaism, but only 4.4 million people in the United States say they practice Judaism.

There is another way of looking at what I have called a disaster in the making. Of the 6.8 million people who are Jews or of Jewish descent, 1.1 million say they have no religion and 1.3 million have joined another religion, adding up to 2.4 million. This means that *one-third of the people in America of Jewish ethnic origin no longer report Judaism as their current religion.*[25] No wonder sociologists and demographers say the debate between optimists and pessimists is over. No wonder a study for the American Jewish Committee concludes that whether the Jewish community "can command the will and resources to support the network of Jewish institutions, causes, and activities within the community, in American society and politics, and abroad, is an open question."[26] If a community establishes institutions fit for a population of five or six million but falls to half that number, who will pay for empty offices, meeting rooms, and synagogues?

Chapter 2

FROM FAITH TO FEAR

DEMOGRAPHIC disasters, of course, do not happen overnight. That now facing American Jewry has roots far into the past, although for a long time they were not really visible.

Jewish life in America began, at least for the vast majority of Jewish families, in the decision of European Jews to leave their parents, their synagogues, and their homes, to go to the New World. That decision was part of a process their descendants now continue: the confrontation between Jews and life in the modern age. Their decision to go to America brought them the challenges that Jews today have inherited: how, and indeed whether, to live as Jews in a society that is overwhelmingly Christian and increasingly secular; what parts of Judaism to cling to and what parts to abandon; whether the community would define itself as Jewish by faith or ethnic inheritance.

At bottom the immigrants faced two questions. Would the American Dream come true for them, so that *Jews* could succeed in America and integrate into the life of this society? And would *Judaism* in America survive that success? Their lives of toil and achievement answered the first question with a resounding yes. The second question lies at the heart of the crisis now facing the American Jewish community.

11

The Sephardim

The earliest Jewish settlers in America were Sephardim, descendants of Jews who had been expelled from Spain in 1492 and had fled to places such as the Ottoman Empire, Holland, and, in the New World, Brazil. They arrived in Dutch and British colonial America, driven to emigrate there by the same forces that propelled other early settlers. In America they soon lived not as poor immigrants in separate neighborhoods but as respected and often prosperous, influential citizens. And they not only mixed with but very often assimilated into the Christian gentry, who accepted them as fellow members of the upper reaches of society. In the South in the early 1800s, "marriage with prominent gentile clans was extensive," one historian reports.[1] In the North it was the same story: "Every Jew who settled and remained in colonial Connecticut before the Revolution married a Christian. Similarly, large numbers of Jews in New York and Philadelphia married, raised their children in the community's dominant faith, and sometimes became Christian themselves."[2]

What was to be the place of Jews in America, as independence approached? These early communities eagerly supported the revolutionary ideals of individual rights and freedom of conscience, which American statesmen learned from the Enlightenment. Viewing themselves not as a community apart but as Americans of Jewish faith, they fought for full citizenship rights and the disestablishment of Christianity as the state religion. At the national level, they shared the victory when the First Amendment to the Constitution was adopted, prohibiting an establishment of religion and guaranteeing them, and all others, the free exercise of their faith. The Jews did not seek to separate religion and society, nor did they argue that the government could not support religion in general. Rather, they demanded that it be absolutely neutral *among* religions. And the Constitution was a great advance toward this goal.

At the state level, however, Jews continued to suffer from disabilities that must have reminded these Sephardim of their experiences in less enlightened regions of Christendom. The constitutions of nine of the thirteen original states contained a reference to Christianity, and four allowed tax assessments for church support. Under the early constitutions of Massachusetts, New Hampshire, New Jersey, North Carolina, Georgia, South Carolina, and Maryland, only Protestants could hold public office. In fact, not until the Civil War was full political equality for American Jews achieved.[3]

The public agenda of American Jews was, then, the demand for equality, and they defined the religious liberty guaranteed in the Constitution as meaning nothing less. They pressed not for a secular state or society but for treatment of Judaism no less favorable than that accorded Christianity. This would be a historic achievement and a sharp break with the past experience of Jew and Christian alike. The strategy of the Jewish community for gaining a secure place in the new United States may be described as insisting on *government neutrality among religions.* But soon, when many new immigrants from Germany arrived, this strategy began to seem inadequate.

Emancipation

The emancipation of Europe's Jews began in Europe itself—in the aftermath of the French Revolution and in the swirl of ideas and actions we call the Enlightenment. For Jews, the Enlightenment, the *Haskalah,* meant throwing off the patterns of life and thought with which they had bound themselves for centuries. It meant a new way of dealing with Christian neighbors and a new relationship with the government, which in many places began to grant Jews more rights as citizens. The first step had been to leave the Jewish settlements and head for the heart of Europe's great cities. This was a physical action for some, coming from shtetls and small towns, and a psychological change for others, who emerged from urban ghettos.

In small towns, in rabbinical courts, and in cities renowned for Jewish learning, Jews in Europe had lived for centuries next to, yet apart from, their Christian neighbors. The Jewish community had not only its own religion but its own language (Yiddish), its own economy, its own system of justice. It had never been entirely cut off from Christian society, and Jews had sold their merchandise to Christians and bought from them the products of the land Jews were forbidden to own. But the Jewish community had enveloped its members and Judaism set the pattern of their days. Its autonomy and its inner peace were broken by the violence of Christian neighbors and Christian princes, seeking taxes and, on occasion, blood.

But in the nineteenth century Jews began to join the social and political, and more of the economic, activities of the people among whom they lived. From the Jewish community emerged philosophers and composers, businessmen and financiers whose lives were played out not within the walls of a ghetto but in the wider life of the country they inhabited.

The first waves of Jewish immigrants from central and eastern Europe arrived from Germany in the 1840s. There had been just a few thousand Sephardic Jews here in the early 1800s, but the German immigration increased their ranks to fifty thousand by 1850, and again to three times that number by 1860. They were escaping the disappointments of a Europe where, especially after the revolutionary hopes of 1848 were dashed, Jews still faced great danger and discrimination. They were also escaping their own pasts, leaving traditional communities governed by Orthodox authorities. It is not surprising that these enterprising and youthful arrivals were drawn from less, rather than more, religious elements of the German Jewish community.

In America, they sought what they could not fully obtain back home: true civil equality for Jews, and a new, more modern kind of Judaism free from the control of Orthodoxy. How could this be achieved? The now enlarged community of American Jews, most originating in Germany, began to envision a new strategy: rather than stand apart as a visibly distinct group and demand government neutrality among religions, it would be wiser to Americanize and assimilate as quickly as possible, and insist that government not support religion at all. So they abandoned German for English and "deliberately downplayed any tendencies that might set them apart from their fellow Americans" in language, dress, and manners, and absolute separation of church and state, not benevolent government support of all religious groups, gradually became the community consensus on public policy.[4]

Their argument for absolute separation was strong. The country they saw before them, and the memories they carried with them, made this seem the logical course to increasing numbers of Jews and their leaders. To begin with, they had experienced government support of established churches in Europe. They did not believe that government would actually remain neutral in any country where the vast majority of citizens were Christian. How would this be possible, when many in the populace, the government, and the churches feared and hated Jews? Any government in a Christian country was certain to propound the "true faith," they believed, if it involved itself in religious matters at all. And if government support for religion must mean support for Christianity, the only way to stop it—to reduce the influence of Christianity on public life and on their lives—was to separate church from state.

This issue arose in disparate areas of life. While full political rights had been won by the time of the Civil War, other battles continued. Must Jews who closed their shops on Saturday close them on Sunday as well? Would there be Bible reading in public schools, and if so, whose Bible? Were Jewish children to be preached to from the New Testament each morning? The only practical answer seemed, again, to keep religious matters out of any contact with the government—and vice versa.

Second, this conclusion was further reinforced by the arrival, just as the German Jews were reaching America, of large numbers of Catholics from Ireland and Germany. Given the historic link between the Catholic Church and anti-Semitism in Europe, it was predictable that Jews would fear to see Catholicism strengthened in America. Far better, again, to ensure that government would do nothing to assist the church.

Third, in Germany Jews who wanted to see reforms of their own faith had often had to face official support for the Orthodox authorities. Separation of church and state meant that the government would leave them to themselves to sort out Jewish community affairs. If the Orthodox rabbinate had no civil authority over Jews, Jews would be free to be irreligious or to define new religious practices they felt more fitting for the modern world. So the popularity of Reform Judaism among the German immigrants also argued for keeping the state out of religious affairs altogether.

Finally, the German Jews arrived here when the goal of previous generations—government neutrality—was already ensconced in the Bill of Rights. They did not have to fight for toleration or legal rights—at least not from the national government. They could raise their sights and ask for more: a society where religion played no public role. For as they became more and more American in their ways, religion alone was what separated them from their fellow citizens. To minimize this divisive factor seemed the safest path.

Moreover, as Naomi Cohen, a leading historian of American Jewry and professor of American Jewish History at the Jewish Theological Seminary, has suggested, as the German Jewish community weakened—in faith, in ritual observance, in cohesiveness—this very weakness led it to hope that the new strategy could substitute for the security Jews no longer obtained from membership in a tightly knit and to some extent self-governing group.[5] Jews were coming to believe that their community might be weaker internally yet safer nonetheless, if the separation between church and state were strengthened while that between Christian and Jew disappeared.

Was there no danger in this approach? Could not a more secular society become a lure to Jews, and lead to the kind of assimilation that had begun to afflict the early Sephardic communities here? Although this argument may have made sense in principle, it could not appear very realistic to Jews of that time and place.

The Jewish community of the early 1900s was now filled with immigrants who—whatever their level of ritual observance—spoke Yiddish, lived among themselves, and were Orthodox at least in their religious training and education. What is more, community solidarity was reinforced by pressure from without, by anti-Semitism. The lynching of Leo Frank by a Georgia mob in 1915 reminded Jews that even in America, anti-Semitism could bring violence and death.

Given the extremely high levels of prejudice and anti-Semitism prevalent then, the foreignness of the newly arrived Jews, and their intense desire to become part of American society, the risk of assimilation evoked far less concern than the challenge of achieving full participation in this new society.

Tired, Poor—and Secular

By the early twentieth century the Jewish community was rapidly being swelled by yet a new immigration: in the decades between 1880 and World War I, millions of poor Jews from Russia and

17

eastern Europe began to reach New York and other East Coast ports. By the end of the war, four million Jews lived in America. While their arrival transformed much in American Jewish life, it only reinforced the view that a secular American society was the safest one for Jews.

For most American Jews, the story begins here—with the arrival, three or four generations back, of a relative from eastern Europe. Like the German Jews, these newcomers were escaping not only government oppression but sometimes family and religious authority as well. For a young Jewish man or woman, the tsar was a distant tyrant; often there were others closer at hand. The vast majority came from observant, indeed Orthodox, families. Here, in America, their Orthodoxy crumbled.

From a religious point of view, the transition from shtetl to life in New York City—or Boston, Chicago, Cleveland, or the other major places of settlement—was devastating. In his famous book about the immigrant experience, *The Rise of David Levinsky,* Abraham Cahan's hero explains that "If you are a Jew of the type to which I belonged when I came to New York and you attempt to bend your religion to the spirit of your new surroundings, it breaks. It falls to pieces. The very clothes I wore and the very food I ate had a fatal effect on my religious habits."[6]

My own maternal grandfather arrived here just before World War I, from the town of Tlumatch in Galicia–then belonging to Austria–Hungary, now part of Ukraine. He and my grandmother had an entirely Orthodox upbringing, and to the day they died their household remained strictly kosher. But when employers required that he work on the Sabbath, my grandfather complied. The synagogue, and religious law, took second place to the need to feed five children. A chain-smoker until his death, he was soon smoking on the Sabbath, too, and by the time I knew him he confined his visits to the synagogue to the High Holidays.

The society operated according to Christian rhythms: Christmas and Easter were work and school holidays, not Rosh Hashanah and Yom Kippur.* Sabbath closing laws shut stores on Sunday, not Saturday. The food, as David Levinsky said, violated Jewish dietary laws, not those of Christians. Toward the end of the nineteenth century a famous European rabbi declared (in Yiddish, of course) that America, which so many Jews called the promised land, was in fact a *"trefe land"*—an unkosher country.[7] Abraham Cahan knew what the rabbi meant. For the Puritans, the New World had provided the opportunity to practice their religion more freely than had the Old, and they saw themselves as the successors to the ancient Hebrews striking out into the wilderness. For the descendants of those Hebrews, life in America, far from reinforcing their religious practices, eroded them.

In addition, the very individualism of the Enlightenment philosophers subverted the spirit of Jewish peoplehood. The free individual choice of which those thinkers wrote, and which was sanctified in the U.S. Constitution, was absolutely contrary to the Jewish idea of covenant and commandment. Jewish law was about the collective, inherited obligation to God of an entire people. Could anything have been further from the modern notion that each individual must freely choose his faith? And could anything have been more subversive of the idea that Jews were by birth bound to 613 commandments than a philosophy suggesting that men were free at birth from any religious obligations whatsoever?

But there is more: something special about Judaism that rendered Jews less able to cope with America than members of other old-world religions. Nathan Glazer, professor emeritus of sociology

---

*Ironically, the United States Holocaust Memorial Museum, in Washington, D.C., is open on Rosh Hashanah and closed on Christmas Day.

at Harvard and author of the classic study *American Judaism,* wisely described the problem:

> Judaism is even more vulnerable to the unsettling influence of modernity than is Christianity. Judaism emphasizes acts, rituals, habits, a way of life. . . . once one had found—as so many immigrants did—that it was more convenient to work on Saturdays or to shave or to abandon traditional dress, one had no body of doctrine to fall back upon that could explain what remained *really* important in Judaism—indeed, the question was whether *anything* was really more important than the rituals established by God's word. Under these circumstances, an entire way of life disintegrated."[8]

Professor Glazer was not suggesting that there are no doctrines in Judaism but rather that eastern European Jews had tended to concentrate on ritual far more than on doctrine. And the eastern European Jews who came to America—the grandparents and great-grandparents of most American Jews—were usually, to say it again, not the most devout people in their communities. Some came for economic opportunity, some to escape the draft, and many to escape oppression, but they did not come to pray. And when they did come to America for religious freedom, very often they were seeking the freedom to be irreligious.

In Europe they had performed the rituals, for there was parental and social pressure to do so, and it was easier to live as a Jew than to violate community norms. But in New York, the reverse was true. There was pressure to grab a (probably nonkosher) sandwich, to work on "Shabbes" (the Sabbath), to skip a prayer here and there. And as the ritual pillars began to collapse, they brought down with them the whole structure of faith for many new American Jews.

Finally, the American Jewish community cannot have been unaffected, in its religious behavior, by its own argument that a secular society was a safer one for Jews. If religious divisions within the society threatened Jews, how could it be helpful to stress them by ritual practices that set Jews apart from their neighbors? In the mid-1880s, the eastern European poet J.L. Gordon, a champion of the *Haskalah,* told his community that the Enlightenment now allowed Jews to join civil society. The formula was to "Be a Jew in your tent and a 'mensch' [a man like any other] when you go out."[9] But Gordon did not foresee that those who stopped being Jews in the street and on the job almost inevitably would stop being Jews in their "tents" as well. An end to rituals that interfered with the rhythms of American life—such as *kashrut* (the dietary laws), strict Sabbath observance, and the wearing of distinctive clothing—might soon undercut faith as well, for who could wish to believe that he was shirking and doing wrong? Far easier, and more natural, to shirk not only the practice but the beliefs that required it. To enjoy the bounty of America fully, to mute the distinctiveness that had always brought danger to Jews, and to contribute to the building of a secular society where Enlightenment values would be safer, all seemed to lead away from traditional Judaism as it had been practiced for a thousand years.

Away from traditional Judaism, and into the melting pot. For nothing was more American than the steady diminution of Old World traditions among the new immigrant groups, and especially among their children. It was nearly unthinkable, and surely un-American, for any group to wall itself off, rejecting the fabulous opportunities of this new land because it preferred self-segregation and absolute fidelity to its past. True, the Amish and a few other sects did this and ultimately earned the admiration of the society at large for their resolute refusal to integrate. But this was a small exception, and the vast sea of immigrants—Jew and Christian alike—embraced the American ethos. Far from segregating themselves from America as the Amish did, the majority of Jews sought the "social invisibility" that alone would protect them and permit them to thrive here.[10]

The Rise of Secularism

By the 1920s there were millions of Jews in America and, as we have seen, they constituted 3.7 percent of the population. Yet there is another way to see that number, and it is the way most Jews, and their leaders, saw it: America was still more than 96 percent Christian. The leaders of the most important Jewish organizations wondered what public policies would best protect American Jews, and faced again the choices that had once been before their predecessors. They could insist that Judaism be given an equal place with Christianity in a deeply religious America, or they could seek a more secular America where religion's role was diminished.

They chose the latter path. Their choice is not in retrospect surprising—nor, even when viewed in the light of today's demographic crisis, was it wrong. They did not believe that even in America, even in the twentieth century, Christians would grant Judaism equal dignity. If there were no religious tests for public office by the late 1800s, American society remained pervasively Christian. Moreover, there were repeated efforts by Christian clergy and activist laymen to push through Congress the so-called "Christian state" amendment, which would push aside the neutrality mandated by the First Amendment and make America an officially Christian country. Judaism would be relegated to a permanently inferior position, and the ability of Jews to succeed in America would suffer enormous damage. How could an officially Christian nation ever be "home" to Jews? Jews strongly opposed and resisted the "Christian staters," as they were known, and even became suspicious of other causes dear to the Christian clergy, such as the temperance movement.[11]

Within the Jewish community, efforts to resist the Christian staters, protect Jewish children from having to recite Christian prayers, or allow observant Jews who closed their stores Saturday for Sabbath observance to open them Sunday despite "Sunday Closing" laws all caused no controversy. For if the principle behind these actions was strict secularism, the actual cases in point were far less radical and far more appealing. They were most often battles not for secularism but for equality and tolerance.

Most American Jewish leaders came to believe that security in America would be found by insisting that this country was meant to be secular, that its Constitution required this outcome, and that Jewish pressures to diminish the role of religion were based not on self-interest but on faith in law and the Constitution. For most of them, there must have seemed to be no alternative to this approach. For what else could they do? Accept permanent inferiority, or assault Christianity and hope to change its view of Jews? The first was morally unacceptable, the second implausible and dangerous.

Old Laws and New

The adoption of this approach fit perfectly with the Jewish attraction to Enlightenment views of social organization and Jewish respect for "The Law."

The universalism of the Enlightenment attracted Jews because it offered them a way out of the ghetto. The two great secular movements that won the support of European Jews after the Enlightenment, socialism and Zionism, had something of Jewish messianism in them. Zionism thought to save the Jews and socialism to save all mankind, and on one question both agreed entirely: it was dangerous for Jews to live as a distinct minority in a Christian state. Dividing religion from state and society, and relegating it exclusively to the area of private life, had been seen by Jews in Europe as the beginning of their emancipation. America was no different from Europe in this respect, for here, too, a society where individuals could make their way without being segregated according to group origins would be better for Jews.

A more secular, more tolerant, more open society would be more just, benefit all minorities, and be truer to the nation's fundamental principles. Those principles were not specifically American but rather universal values such as liberty and equality—precisely the values of the Enlightenment. There was a complete identity among Enlightenment, American, and Jewish values, according to this view.

To this mix was added a new version of the ancient Jewish respect for "The Law," as Jerold S. Auerbach explains in his brilliant work *Rabbis and Lawyers*.[12] A reinterpretation of Judaism's commitment to "The Law" became a critical element of American Jewish adaptation to life in this country, he argues. In essence, Jewish immigrants became American Jews by redefining Judaism and submerging it in Americanism, itself newly defined by the Jewish lawyers who came to lead the community.

In the 1800s rabbis had usually been the community's most influential leaders; but early in this century lawyers such as Louis Marshall, who served as president of the American Jewish Committee, and Louis Brandeis, the first Jew to serve on the Supreme Court, took their place. "As they redefined Jewish legitimacy in American legal terms," Auerbach recounts, "they fused Torah and Constitution as the sacred texts of a Judeo-American legal tradition."[13] A key conduit was America's Puritan heritage, which permitted connecting ancient Israel and America "to a common democratic tradition whose origins could be found in the Hebrew Bible."[14] The Puritans looked back to ancient Israel, and the Jews used that reference to affirm their own new American identity. The "new synthesis" that Marshall and Brandeis developed between

1906 and 1916 was based on the importance of law and justice in both the American and the Jewish traditions.[15] The result was

> the identification of Judaism with Americanism. . . . The prophetic teachings of 'brotherhood and righteousness' . . . had become the modern liberal ideals of democracy and social justice.[16]

As Brandeis put it, "the highest Jewish ideals are essentially American," for "America's fundamental law seeks to make real the brotherhood of man. That brotherhood became the Jews' fundamental law more than twenty-five hundred years ago."[17]

Under the leadership of Marshall and Brandeis, Auerbach concludes, "the rule of law that governed American Jewish life came to depend upon the Constitution, not the Torah."[18] This sacralization of the Constitution joined Judaism and Americanism, and immigrant Jews were now able to embrace a synthesis that allowed them to be patriotic Americans as well as observant Jews—observant, that is, of the newly defined requirements and responsibilities of the Jew in America.

Safety through secularism, integration rather than separatism, and life under the new sacred Law of the Constitution rather than the old Law of the Torah became the American Jewish ideology, and the institutions of the community pursued it with zeal. By the 1960s the battle to disestablish Christianity as the nation's public religion had largely been won. Great public occasions required clergymen from all three denominations—Protestant, Catholic, and Jewish—and the inadmissibility of using state power to advance Christianity was well established. Still the Jewish community pressed on, as Naomi Cohen reported in her history of the American Jewish Committee.

> Jewish insistence on the sanctity of separation persisted. . . . as a pluralistic society accepted Jewish assertiveness more readily, the Jewish mi-

nority sharpened its attack against any entering wedge, no matter how innocuous in itself, which might breach the wall of separation.[19]

Over the decades, as eastern European Jews became dominant in American Jewish life, the major Jewish organizations changed from being creatures of the rich, assimilated German Jewish elites who saw themselves as stewards of the community. But the ideology of these organizations, which was secularist and non-Orthodox, did not change as their leadership passed from civic-minded laymen to a new generation of professionals. The members of this new group, like their more elitist predecessors, were highly secular in their own private lives and unenthusiastic about the role of religion in American society: "They spoke for a religious community, but . . . their actions in opposition to public religion reflected their own indifference if not hostility to religion itself."[20] This is not an idiosyncratic assessment: a history of the Synagogue Council of America concluded that the major philanthropic and defense organizations were "administered by lay and professional leaders whose attitude toward the Jewish religion ranged from simple indifference to open hostility."[21]

Kiryas Joel, Rosenberger, and the Separationist Faith

Originally, for example, the Jewish defense organizations fought to remove Christian prayers from the public schools on the ground of discrimination against Jewish children. But when specifically Christian prayers were gone, these organizations carried on the fight, hoping to exclude *any* prayer (even voluntary and silent prayer), any observance of religious holidays, any benediction at graduation ceremonies, or any use of school facilities by religious groups.[22] In one celebrated case, Jewish organizations sided with a school administration that permitted all voluntary student clubs to use school facilities after school was out at 3:00 P.M.—except a Bible club.[23] This, the students argued, was discrimination against only one form of voluntary student activity, Bible study. But the school administration resisted, and the major Jewish organizations supported it and sought to bar even this after-hours and unofficial religious activity. The principle they backed was absolutism in the separation of church and state, for fear that any link of religion to a public institution would eventually endanger American Jews.

Soon, however, that principle was extended from church and state to religion and society. Separation of church and state, as the late social critic Christopher Lasch put it, is "nowadays interpreted as prohibiting any public recognition of religion at all."[24] While the Supreme Court has been rethinking these questions recently, the major Jewish organizations continue faithfully to promote the absolutist dogma.

This continuing effort is perfectly illustrated by the 1994 case involving the Kiryas Joel school district. Kiryas Joel is a town in New York State established in 1977 and populated by twelve thousand members of the Satmar sect of Hasidic Jews. The problem they faced when they established their private religious school system was the burden of educating emotionally and physically disabled children. When the sect's leaders concluded that they lacked the resources to educate these children, they tried to arrange for their education at the expense of the state—invoking a right common to all New Yorkers. The children were, for a time, educated in secular subjects by licensed public school teachers on premises within the town. Later, state authorities said this solution violated separation of church and state, and insisted that the disabled children be transported to public school premises outside the town. Claiming that the trip away from familiar surroundings upset the children, and that the other students who crossed their paths mocked their distinctive clothing and appearance, the parents convinced the state legislature

to establish the town as a separate school district so that their handicapped children could be educated at a public school within it. The
only schooling offered by this new school district was a secular
special education program for handicapped children, and the teachers, therapists, and district superintendent were not Satmar Hasidim
and did not reside in the town. Still, the state superintendent of
schools brought suit, arguing that this new school district was set up
solely to help the Hasidim and as such constituted an unconstitutional establishment of religion.

As might be expected, the major Jewish organizations (with the
exception of the Union of Orthodox Jewish Congregations, Agudath Israel of America, and the National Council of Young Israel—
all Orthodox groups) lined up uniformly against the Hasidim.
Instead, an amicus curiae brief was filed by the Anti-Defamation
League, the American Jewish Committee, and the National Council
of Jewish Women, together with the American Civil Liberties
Union, the Unitarian Universalist Association, and Americans
United for Separation of Church and State; another brief was joined
by the Union of American Hebrew Congregations, the American
Jewish Congress, and the National Jewish Community Relations
Advisory Council with People for the American Way. Outside of Or-
thodox Jews, the only organizations who sided with the Hasidim
were the National Association of Evangelicals and the U.S. Catholic
Conference.

As to the arguments made, the UAHC-AJCongress-NJCRAC-
People for the American Way brief ended with a statement on its
final page revealing its authors' real concern:

CONCLUSION: These are perilous times for common school education. The very idea of a common school is under broad attack. . . . KJSD
[Kiryas Joel School District] dismisses the unfairness of creating a

school district for this religious community. It suggests that no other group is likely to be as seriously affected. The claim ignores the many religious communities intensely dissatisfied with the public schools over creationism, outcome based education, sex education, and "secular humanism." They (and their opponents) would be happy to create fiefdoms of religious or non-religious homogeneity if this Court confers its constitutional blessings on KJSD.[25]

The deep religious faith of the Kiryas Joel Hasidim was for the major Jewish organizations outweighed by their fear that some conservative or fundamentalist Christian groups might conceivably benefit from a Kiryas Joel victory.

Thus separation of church and state has here taken another step, for now it appeared that any state action whose effect is to help parents keep their children faithful to their religious beliefs could be struck down as unconstitutional. The major Jewish groups were all arguing this—that to assist Orthodox Jews in making their children Orthodox Jews was *by definition* unconstitutional. Several members of the Supreme Court agreed. New York's law went beyond constitutional bounds, Justice Stevens wrote in his opinion, because it "provided official support to cement the attachment of young adherents to a particular faith" and in this sense "affirmatively supports a religious sect's interest in segregating itself and preventing its children from associating with their neighbors."

This language is a far cry from the ways in which the Court used to talk about religious obligations and the parental role. In the famous 1925 case *Pierce v. Society of Sisters,* the Court spoke of "the rights of parents to direct the rearing and education of their children," and in a 1944 case it added that

It is cardinal with us that the custody, care, and nurture of the child reside first in the parents, whose primary function and freedom include the preparation for obligations the state can neither hinder nor supply.[26]

If these decisions do not speak to the issue of public aid to parochial schools, they do demonstrate how the Court's attitude toward parents who seek to bind their children into obligatory religious commitments has changed—from respect and even admiration to outright hostility. And in this journey the Court had the support of most American Jewish organizations.

Judaism, because it is an all-embracing way of life—intended to govern or at least influence one's thoughts and behavior from waking until sleep, and from birth until death—cannot be entirely private, in that it affects one's behavior in society. Nor is it entirely voluntary, for the Jew is born into a covenantal community with obligations to God.

But the view of the Jewish agencies—and to some extent of the Court majority, which decided against the Hasidim—is very distant from this understanding: It is that religion is not a way of life, but rather a private opinion. As Nathan Lewin, an Orthodox Jew who was the attorney for the Kiryas Joel Hasidim, noted, the justices "do not see religion as an individual lifelong condition, like poverty or disability. They view it as a temporary personal preference—a possession that one may choose to keep or discard."[27] Far from being a network of obligatory actions that must be taken to follow God's commandments, religion becomes just another "life-style choice." Any adjustment to that personal preference, then, is an unconstitutional favoring of religion, and Justice Souter called the Kiryas Joel law unconstitutional "religious favoritism."

This is the attitude Yale law professor Steven Carter, in his recent book *The Culture of Disbelief,* called seeing "religion as a hobby."

But this formulation, though fetching, is not quite adequate. It explains the Court's tendency to dismiss religious commitments as a matter of personal preference deserving of little respect or accommodation but does not really get to the heart of the matter: for who, after all, is against hobbies? For Lewin, there was "nothing constitutionally dubious in accommodating religion by granting secular respect to the fact that religion is extremely important to some people, and they should be accorded latitude in the private observance of their faith."[28] But despite the fact that they represent a small minority religion that has throughout history had to fight for the right to practice its tenets freely, this view was rejected by the major Jewish organizations. They adhered instead to that old injunction to "Be a Jew in your tent and a mensch when you go out," showing little sympathy to Jews who insisted on proclaiming their Judaism even when "outside the tent."

Far from demanding that the government grant some leeway to facilitate the practice of a demanding faith, in this case their own, the Jewish groups insisted that such an accommodation is *not only unwise but unlawful.* The elements of the Jewish community having the greatest difficulty keeping their children Jewish used the courts to attack the practice by which the elements having the greatest success keeping their children Jewish were doing so.

Then in 1995, the Supreme Court stepped back from the ever more absolute separationist position it seemed to be embracing in *Kiryas Joel.* In two cases, *Capitol Square Review and Advisory Board v. Pinette* and *Rosenberger v. Rector and Visitors of the University of Virginia,*[29] the Court refused to read an endorsement of religion into official actions treating religious activity no better and no worse than other forms of private conduct. In *Capitol Square,* the issue was whether the Ku Klux Klan could erect a cross on the grounds of the Ohio state capitol, in an area where private groups were allowed to demonstrate, speak, and otherwise present their views.

Previously, Christmas trees and Hanukkah menorahs, for example, had been erected on the Capitol Square grounds. Was this a violation of the Establishment Clause of the First Amendment, because some passers-by might think the state had erected the display and was fostering Christianity, Judaism, or religion in general?

In *Rosenberger*, students at the University of Virginia paid $14 per semester to a Student Activities Fund that supported various student clubs and publications. These included a satirical anti-Christian paper called the *Yellow Journal*, the Jewish Law Students Association, the Muslim Students Association, the Gay and Lesbian Law Students Association, and various environmental, abortion rights, animal rights, and other clubs and journals. The Student Activities Fund did not give any student journals money directly but paid the company that printed them. University officials refused to permit payments to the printer for one publication, *Wide Awake*, which was avowedly Christian, on the grounds that this would be state support for religion barred by the Constitution.

In *Capitol Square,* the Court decided that the cross was private religious speech protected by the First Amendment, for the state did not sponsor it. To permit all private groups, including religious groups, access to this location does not aid religion, while permitting everyone access except religious groups would discriminate against them. The Court was divided as to whether it matters that passers-by might erroneously believe the state was endorsing religion, but in any event concluded that a reasonable person would not think so.

In *Rosenberger*, the journal *Wide Awake* was refused funding, the Court said, because the university examined its content and decided that student journalistic efforts with religious viewpoints would be disallowed. This was a violation of "vital First Amendment speech principles." Would the university, the Court asked, bar "hypothetical student contributors named Plato, Spinoza, and Descartes" on the same grounds? The Court's opinion concluded that "the governmental program here is neutral toward religion" in part because the student fees are not "a tax levied for the direct support of a church" and "no public funds flow directly to [*Wide Awake's*] coffers." The program "respects the critical difference 'between government speech endorsing religion, which the Establishment Clause forbids, and private speech endorsing religion, which the Free Speech and Free Exercise Clauses protect.'"

In these cases the Court took a clear step back from the extremes of separationism, provided a bit more space for religious views in the 'public square,' and clarified a point it had previously made—that the Establishment Clause does not require barring religious viewpoints from expression in neutral government programs. *But the major Jewish organizations refused to take that step back.* They fought the Court's conclusions, once again joining with the absolute separatist groups submitting briefs. In *Capitol Square,* one brief was filed jointly by Americans United for Separation of Church and State, People for the American Way, the ACLU, the Union of American Hebrew Congregations, and the American Jewish Committee, and it argued that the cross should be ruled unconstitutional because it "would create the appearance" that the state was endorsing religion even if it actually was not. A brief filed jointly by the ADL and the American Jewish Congress argued this same point. Even if the state was not supporting the religious display, their brief insisted, and even if reasonable passers-by would understand this, "it is sufficient, as we will emphasize again, that a 'reasonable observer' might draw the inference [of official endorsement], or, indeed, that *some* portion of the reasonable observers in the community might so infer."[30]

In other words, the constitutional rights to freedom of religious speech and free exercise of religion were to be denied here, and not because government was *actually* supporting or endorsing religion but rather because some observers might *mistakenly* think the government backed the display. Thus the major Jewish groups twisted and turned to stop any public displays of religion.

In *Rosenberger* as well, the Jewish organizations took the absolutist line, arguing that *Wide Awake* must be excluded from the student fund because this case involved "a direct cash subsidy" from the state, and "when the government pays the bills, it is no longer granting access, it is actually advancing the religious message."[31] This argument constituted a special demonstration of their extreme desire to fight the funding: even to the extreme of being factually wrong. As the Supreme Court noted, "no public funds flow directly to [*Wide Awake*'s] coffers."

The major non-Orthodox Jewish organizations rejected such deviations from absolute separationism. Not for them was the Court's effort to find some space in the "public square" for religion, nor for them the careful factual distinctions that some of the justices relied upon. They still see the expression of religious convictions as a danger to Jews. Whatever may be the nature of their commitment to Judaism, their faith in separationism is absolutely intact.

Secularism and Safety

The strategy of the American Jewish community presupposes that any expression of religious faith or association is dangerous to American Jewry. As such, it must be resisted—whatever the ostensible grounds.

Thus the official views of the Jewish community in the 1992 Rhode Island benediction case, *Lee v. Weisman,* where the Supreme Court found that it was unconstitutional for a rabbi to read a prayer at a high school commencement. The case was brought by a nonreligious Jewish family, the Weismans, whose daughter Deborah was a graduating senior. A majority of five justices found that her objections to the prayer were enough to make it impermissible as a matter of government coercion. She might be made to feel uncomfortable by this prayer reading, and might feel peer pressure to stand during the prayer or in some other way show a belief in God that she did not have. This was the "coercion" that rendered the prayer unconstitutional in the view of five of the nine justices. Justice Kennedy wrote, in the opinion of the Court, that "the undeniable fact is that the school district's supervision and control of a high school graduation ceremony places public pressure, as well as peer pressure, on attending students to stand as a group or, at least, maintain respectful silence during the Invocation and Benediction." This could not be allowed because "research in psychology supports the common assumption that adolescents are often susceptible to pressure from their peers towards conformity."[32]

So the benediction was barred, because it was too much to ask Ms. Weisman to stand quietly or sit silently when others prayed.[33] The support of Jewish organizations for Ms. Weisman's cause, and their jubilation at her victory, were the product of their assessment of American society and the Jewish place in it. The tradition of benedictions at great public events, from a presidential inauguration to a high school commencement, goes back to the founding of the Republic, but they found it an offensive and unconstitutional practice. In their arguments to the Supreme Court, they once again remained true to the strategy that has motivated them for decades. In other words, they continue to believe that a secular America is the only safe America for Jews, and to oppose any practice that may force American Jews to acknowledge their religion in public—or permit Christians to do so. They continue to believe that these results are compelled by sacred law, in this case the Constitution.

The foregoing cases provide striking evidence of what is actually a shift in the thinking of America's Jewish "leaders." From the original Jewish insistence that Judaism be treated with the respect accorded to other religions, and even beyond the subsequent belief that any form of government support for religion was barred by the Constitution and potentially harmful to American Jews, their position presently stands revealed not merely as fear of government support for religion but *fear of religion itself.* They see religion not as the guarantor of civic virtue but as the source of civic strife—and of danger for Jews.

Why have Jews come to believe this? Because in their view a greater role for religion in American life means an increasingly Christian, and accordingly less hospitable, environment. Their fear of this is to a very great extent heightened by the growth of evangelical Christianity and the so-called Christian right, for Jews wonder what place they would be allotted in the America those groups have been characterized as wishing to create.

Chapter 3

THE GOSPEL ABOUT JEWS

J EWS BROUGHT with them to America the memory of Christian Jew-hatred, and one or two generations on, many Jews continue to harbor "an intense fear of the vision of a Christian America."[1] Every sign of vitality and self-assertion that appears among religious Christians arouses apprehension among them. They fear that if religion is to have a greater role in American life, Jews must live in an increasingly Christian, and therefore less welcoming, society.

The origins of this, of course, lie in the bloody two-thousand-year history of Christian anti-Semitism. Throughout almost all that period, Christianity taught contempt for Judaism as a desiccated religion of fanatical formalism, superseded by the coming of Jesus and in essence dead after Jesus' death. Jews were also—at various times and with varying degrees of violence—presented as the killers of Jesus whom God had cursed for this crime, ending His covenant with Abraham. Christian religious activism, whether connected to an epochal event like the Crusades or to annual celebrations like Easter, had throughout European history been the occasion of anti-Semitic violence.

So deep is the visceral response to this history of Christian anti-Semitism that even a figure like Rabbi Leon Klenicki, who supervises interfaith programs at the Anti-Defamation League of B'nai

B'rith—a leading Jewish defense agency—and whose lifework is dedicated to interfaith dialogue, cannot shake it.

> I see it every time I leave the synagogue. On Saturday morning after services, while going home, it is there, waiting for me, challenging me. It is the cross of a nearby church. Why does it disturb me?
>
> The fact is that Jews tend to view the Shoah [Holocaust] as the culmination of their degradation and persecution at the hand of the Christians. They see Christians by and large as persecutors.[2]

Of course most of this persecution, and all the worst of it, had taken place in Europe rather than America. In America violence was limited to the acts of individual roughnecks rather than state-supported pogroms, and the obstacles Jews faced eroded in the decades after World War II. Though it may seem remarkable, despite their enormous successes in America and despite the remarkable social integration between Jews and Christians, Jews even today still fear the impact of Christianity and the actions of its most devout followers.

This is what makes it critical to understand what is *in fact* now being said about Jews and Judaism by American Christians. Is the fear held by so many American Jews justified, or does it constitute a willful ignorance of developments in Christian conceptions of Judaism? Is it informed by knowledge—or largely by prejudice?

A Revolution in Christian Views of Judaism

Whatever the millennia-long Jewish experience of Christianity, however, the fact is that Christian views of Judaism are changing. Christians are confronting Christianity's past—a reexamination of Christian teaching about Jews that, in the words of Leonard Dinnerstein, is "one of the most far-reaching breakthroughs, and one with potential for enormous change in Christian beliefs and behavior."[3] The Jewish community, however, by and large is paying this epochal undertaking no attention. As Rabbi Mordecai Waxman, a former president of the Synagogue Council of America, stated, "Jews who are in professional contact with Christians are aware of recent changes. The average Jew, however, is not as yet particularly cognizant of the new climate which, after all, arises out of the esoteric realm of theology."[4]

Thus while the changes in Christian attitudes are profound, they so far seem to be making little impression on America's Jews. Moreover, a review of Jewish writings about Christianity would be short and not very significant. For though living Christians are very important to living Jews, the truth is that in the theological sense, Christianity is not important to Judaism.

Obversely, Christian texts of course deal extensively with the Hebrew Bible and the meaning of Judaism during Jesus' time, and Catholic and Protestant educational materials contain innumerable references to Jews and the Hebrew Bible (of which some, as we shall see, are quite objectionable to Jews). What, then, is the nature of the Christian revisions?

The Roman Catholic Church

Since the Second Vatican Council began to reevaluate Catholic teaching about Jews and Judaism in 1965, the changes have been revolutionary. Rabbi James Rudin, director of interreligious affairs at the American Jewish Committee, summed it up: "Theologically, we've resolved everything with the Catholics."[5]

The 1965 declaration *Nostra Aetate* stressed the church's origins in and close relationship to Judaism. It stated that "the Jews remain very dear to God," abandoning the Church Fathers' ancient view that they had been rejected by Him. Indeed, *Nostra Aetate* stated that Jews continue to have their own special relationship to God. It also clearly rejected the charge of deicide, and as clearly condemned anti-Semitism.

The implications of *Nostra Aetate* were enormous for Catholic teaching, and the church began to think them through. Nine years later, in 1974, came the Vatican's *Guidelines and Suggestions for Implementing the Conciliar Declaration* Nostra Aetate. Here the church added references to the "rich" developments in Judaism in the post-biblical period, and suggested that Catholics should "strive to learn by what essential traits the Jews define themselves in the light of their own religious experience." These two changes were critical. The first jettisoned the argument that Judaism had lost its raison d'être and its relationship with God when Jesus was born, acknowledging that Judaism was very much alive. The second told Catholics to evaluate Judaism not simply from the Catholic viewpoint but from that of the Jews themselves.

In 1985, the Vatican Commission for Religious Relations with the Jews produced *Notes on the Correct Way to Present Jews and Judaism in Preaching and Catechesis in the Roman Catholic Church.* Here the church took up the anti-Semitic, or anti-Judaic, language in some of the Gospels. (Matthew 27:25, for example, has the Jews saying "His blood be on us and our children.") The *Notes* stated that the Gospels were "the outcome of long and complicated editorial work. . . . Hence it cannot be ruled out that some references hostile or less than favorable to the Jews have their historical context in conflicts between the nascent Church and the Jewish community. Certain controversies reflect Christian-Jewish relations long after the time of Christ."[6] Thus hostility to Jews was demoted from "gospel truth" and put in its historical context.

The Notes also underscored the religious significance of what Christians call the Old Testament and Jews call the Torah, or Hebrew Bible, saying it "retains its own value as revelation." And, like the 1974 *Guidelines,* it reaffirmed that Judaism is a living religion:

The history of Israel did not end in 70 A.D. It continued, especially in a numerous Diaspora which allowed Israel to carry to the whole world a witness—often heroic—of its fidelity to the one God and to 'exalt God in the presence of all the living' while preserving the memory of the land of their forefathers at the heart of their hope. . . . The permanence of Israel . . . is a historic fact and a sign to be interpreted within God's design.

Far from viewing Judaism's demise as God's will, the church now portrayed its survival as part of the divine plan. Jewish faithfulness to Judaism, once seen as the obstinate refusal to accept Jesus, was now "heroic." Finally, the *Notes* declared that Catholic educational materials should convey these ideas, and should cover the Holocaust as well.

The *Notes* reflected the views of Pope John Paul II on the subject of Judaism, and he has been a key source and motivator of the Catholic rethinking. The covenant between God and the Jews, he said in the Mainz, Germany, synagogue in 1980, "has never been revoked."[7] The new catechism of the Catholic Church reflects this understanding when it states that "The Jewish faith, unlike other non-Christian religions, is already a response to God's revelation in the Old Covenant."[8] In the Rome Synagogue, he said in 1986 that "With Judaism . . . we have a relationship we do not have with any other religion. You are our dearly beloved brothers and, in a certain way, it could be said that you are our elder brothers." "It is not lawful to say that the Jews are repudiated or cursed," he went on, for "the Jews are beloved of God, who called them with an irrevocable calling."[9] And in 1987 he told the Jewish community in Warsaw that "you continue your particular vocation, showing yourselves to be still the heirs to that election to which God is faithful."[10] Finally, it is far from coincidental that the Vatican and the state of Israel formally recognized each other during his pontificate, exchanging ambassadors in a ceremony over which he presided.

Meanwhile, the Catholic Church was reviewing its attitude toward proselytization of Jews. In 1977 a study paper, "The Mission and Witness of the Church," was presented at the sixth meeting of the liaison committee between the Roman Catholic Church and the International Jewish Committee for Interreligious Consultations. The paper held that while bearing "witness" to the power of God and of the Catholic faith is a religious obligation for Catholics, it should be carried out primarily through living a Christian life. Proselytism—the active effort to convert people to Christianity—is different.

> The Church clearly rejects every form of unwarranted proselytism. Excluded, then, is every kind of testimony and preaching that in any way becomes a physical, moral, psychological or cultural constraint on the Jews. . . . Excluded also is every kind of disqualifying judgment, contempt or prejudice that could be levelled against the Jewish people or individual Jews as such, or against their faith, their worship, their culture in general and their religious culture in particular, against their past or present history, their existence and the meaning of their existence. Excluded also are odious types of discussions . . . which try to exalt the Christian religion or Christianity as such by discrediting the Jewish religion and Judaism, whether past or present. We are reminded also of the rejection of any action that aims at changing the religious faith of the Jews. . . . Particularly excluded is any such action or behavior directed towards children, old people, the sick, or adolescents still searching for their place in society. Still more is excluded every kind of threat and coercion.[11]

And it raised the issue of targeting Jews for conversion efforts, and spoke plainly: "the temptation to create organizations of any kind, especially for education or social assistance, to 'convert' Jews, is to be rejected."[12]

In the United States, the National Conference of Catholic Bishops pushed ahead along the same lines. In 1988, the Conference's "Criteria for the Evaluation of Dramatizations of the Passion" addressed dramatizations and textbooks portraying Jesus' death. Historically, Easter was in Europe a time of anti-Semitic pogroms and other violence, stirred up by passion plays with emotional depictions of Jews plotting the murder of Jesus. The bishops demanded that depictions of Jesus' death be purged of all anti-Semitic content. Jesus and his followers were now to be shown as "Jews among Jews"; the "blood curse" of Matthew 27:25 could not be used at all; "Jesus and the disciples must not be set dramatically in opposition to his people, the Jews"; and "Jews should not be depicted as avaricious . . . bloodthirsty . . . or implacable enemies of Christ. . . . Any crowd or questioning scene . . . should reflect the fact that some in the crowd and among the Jewish leaders . . . supported Jesus and that the rest were manipulated by his opponents."

In 1988, the bishops published *God's Mercy Endures Forever: Guidelines on the Presentation of Jews and Judaism in Catholic Teaching.* There was more here about "Holy Week: The Passion Narratives." The *Guidelines* instructed,

> Because of the tragic history of the "Christ-killer" charge as providing a rallying cry over the centuries, a strong and careful homiletic stance is necessary to combat its lingering effects today. Homilists and catechists should seek to provide a proper context for the proclamation of the passion narratives. . . . To the extent that Christians over the centuries made Jews the scapegoats for Christ's death, they drew themselves away from the paschal mystery.

The Guidelines continued with the point that

> the readings of the Easter season. . .require particular attention from the homilist. . . . Some of these readings from Acts . . . can leave an

impression of collective Jewish responsibility for the crucifixion. . . .
In such cases, the homilist should put before the assembly the teachings
of *Nostra Aetate*. . . . statements about Jewish responsibility have to
be kept in context. This is part of the reconciliation between Jews
and Christians to which we are all called.

The document covered the preaching and teaching during the
rest of the year as well:

Consistently affirm the value of the whole Bible. . . . Communicate a
reverence for the Hebrew Scriptures and avoid an approach that reduces
them to a propaedeutic or background for the New Testament. . . . Emphasize the Jewishness of Jesus and his teachings. . . . Respect the continuing validity of God's covenant with the Jewish people and their
responsive faithfulness, despite centuries of suffering, to the divine call
that is theirs.

Moreover, in recent years, the church has produced several books
in conjunction with the Anti-Defamation League of B'nai B'rith
and aimed at teachers and students in Catholic schools. These include *Understanding the Jewish Experience,* in 1978, and *Abraham
Our Father* in 1979. In 1987 came *Within Context: Guidelines for
the Catechetical Presentation of Jews and Judaism in the New Testament,* prepared in an effort to put into practical effect the Vatican's
Notes of 1985. Taken together, these works demonstrate that the
Vatican's and bishops' statements were not mere words but the beginning of a real effort to change the thinking of Roman Catholics
about Jews and Judaism. As Eugene Fisher of the U.S. Catholic
Conference has written, "the 'delivery system' of the Church in implementing the breakthrough declaration, *Nostra Aetate,* is working
to change American Catholic textbooks quite profoundly, if not
with dizzying rapidity."[13]

It is fair to ask whether these new teachings are reflected in Catholic school classrooms and educational materials. The short answer is yes. The first study of Catholic school texts, performed in the 1950s by the American Jewish Committee, found egregious treatment of Jews and Judaism. The texts spoke of the Jews' "obstinacy" and "hypocrisy," blamed them for Jesus' death, and quoted the infamous "His blood be upon us and our children" from Matthew 27:25. There were considerable improvements after Vatican II in 1965, and the trend continues.[14] A good example is a recent comparison of the 1970 and 1986 versions of title headings for the study of Romans 9-11 in the New American Bible, "the version most likely to be found in Catholic homes, schools, and rectories."[15] The 1970 version had a section called "Israel's Present Rejection," but the new heading for that section is "Jews and Gentiles in God's Plan." "Grief for the Jews" is replaced by "Paul's Love for Israel." "Israel's Unbelief" has become "Righteousness Based on Faith," and "Partial Rejection of Israel" is now "The Remnant of Israel."

A comprehensive study of Catholic school textbooks was published in 1995 by Philip A. Cunningham in *Education for Shalom*. Cunningham examined 1,867 primary and 936 secondary school lessons. He found, in general, considerable improvement over previous years, although real problems remained. There were still references to Jewish "legalism" as compared with a Christian emphasis on love and faith, and some polemical biblical passages were used without much explanation or context: "the most important single deficiency in present textbooks is the minimal application or complete lack of critical biblical insights when dealing with New Testament polemic."[16] Nevertheless, Cunningham concluded with respect to primary school textbooks that "there was improvement . . . in every significant period and theme category."[17]

As to secondary schools, he judged that "the secondary series presented a positive picture of Jews and Judaism," and that references to modern Jewish life were "extremely positive. . . . It was clear that the religious life of modern Jews was held in high esteem. . . . It was made clear to both students and teachers that Jesus and his relatives were all Jews."[18]

The hierarchic structures of Roman Catholic religious life make it possible to transmit new and much more positive views of Judaism to the diocesan level. And though there is much yet to be done to ensure that these new messages are conveyed at the classroom level and in each parish, the church has reevaluated Judaism and the change is truly profound. As time passes, and as texts are rewritten and older priests are replaced by younger generations whose education has been based on this new comprehension of Judaism, the process will accelerate.

The "Mainline" Protestant World

The so-called mainline Protestant denominations have undertaken a significant reevaluation of their understanding of Judaism as well. The first steps were taken in Germany, no doubt as a reaction to the Holocaust. In 1950, the Evangelical Lutheran Church in Germany called on all Christian churches to resist anti-Semitism and declared that "God's promise is valid for his Chosen People, even after the crucifixion of Jesus Christ."[19] As in the case of Catholicism, this was a rejection of the age-old Christian view of Judaism as a "dead" religion and an affirmation of its continuing relationship with God.

While there were various developments in Europe,[20] perhaps the first major statement in the United States came from the General Conference of the United Methodist Church in 1972. A "Statement on Inter-religious Dialogue: Jews and Christians" asserted that Jews were still a "covenanted people." It went on to say that "The heritage and hopes of a religious Israel in the context of which Jesus labored have continued to live in the Jewish faith and people," clearly contradicting negative views of Jewish religious life. The statement was also definite on anti-Semitism and Christian responsibility for it: "The persecution by Christians of Jews throughout centuries calls for clear repentance and resolve to repudiate past injustice and to seek its elimination in the present."[21]

The American Lutheran Church, which had already issued a new declaration about relations with Jews in 1971,[22] spoke again in 1974. Its General Convention issued a statement on "The ALC and the Jewish Community" in which it said that "it is undeniable that Christian people have initiated and acquiesced in persecution. Whole generations of Christians have looked with contempt upon this people . . . on the false charge of deicide. Christians ought to acknowledge with repentance and sorrow their part in this tragic history of estrangement."[23]

The statement then took up the particular history of Lutheranism and initiated a criticism of Luther himself.

American Lutherans are the heirs of a long history of prejudicial discrimination against Jews. . . . Lutherans bear a special responsibility for this tragic history of persecution, because the Nazi movement found a climate of hatred already in existence. . . . That the Nazi period fostered a revival of Luther's own medieval hostility toward Jews . . . is a special cause of regret. Those who study and admire Luther should acknowledge unequivocally that his anti-Jewish writings are beyond any defense.[24]

The statement noted continuing divisions among Lutherans as to whether there remained a "mission" to convert Jews that went beyond the call for mere dialogue between Lutherans and Jews.

It is unrealistic to expect that Lutherans will think alike or speak with one voice on the motive and method of bearing witness to their Jewish neighbors. Some Lutherans find in Scripture clear directives to bear missionary witness in which conversion is hoped for. Others hold that when Scripture speaks about the relation between Jews and Christians its central theme is that God's promises to Israel have not been abrogated.[25]

The most recent Lutheran statement came in 1994 from the Evangelical Lutheran Church in America, into which the American Lutheran Church had merged, and it powerfully addressed the issue of Christian anti-Semitism. "The Declaration of the Evangelical Lutheran Church in America to the Jewish Community," adopted April 18, 1994, by the Church Council, stated that

> In the long history of Christianity there exists no more tragic development than the treatment accorded the Jewish people on the part of Christian believers. . . . Lutherans belonging to the Lutheran World Federation and the Evangelical Lutheran Church in America feel a special burden in this regard because of certain elements in the legacy of the reformer Martin Luther.

As to Luther, it continued that "we who bear his name and heritage must with pain acknowledge also Luther's anti-Judaic diatribes and violent recommendations of his later writings against the Jews. . . . we reject this violent invective, and yet more do we express our deep and abiding sorrow over its tragic effects on subsequent generations."

It concluded that "we express our urgent desire to live out our faith in Jesus Christ with love and respect for the Jewish people. We recognize in anti-Semitism a contradiction and an affront to the Gospel, a violation of our hope and calling, and we pledge this church to oppose the deadly working of such bigotry, both within our own circles and in the society around us."

This is a powerful, emotional document. Dr. Franklin Sherman, director of the Institute for Jewish-Christian Understanding at the Lutheran Church-related Muhlenberg College, commented that "Lutherans understand the depth of this matter—that the 'teaching of contempt' is not just one mistake among others, but in the whole history of Christianity is the darkest stain upon the Christian faith and the Christian community."[26]

Several other denominational statements are noteworthy, both for their content and for an understanding of just how widespread are the new attitudes to Judaism. The United Church of Christ, in 1987 and 1990, issued statements about Jews and their religion and about Christian anti-Semitism. In 1987, the 16th General Synod adopted a resolution on "The Relationship Between United Church of Christ and the Jewish Community":

> We in the United Church of Christ acknowledge that the Christian Church has, throughout much of its history, denied God's continuing covenantal relationship with the Jewish people expressed in the faith of Judaism. This denial often has led to outright rejection of the Jewish people and to theologically and humanly intolerable violence. The Church's frequent portrayal of the Jews as blind, recalcitrant, evil, and rejected by God has found expression in much Christian theology, liturgy, and education. Such a negative portrayal of the Jewish people and of Judaism has been a factor in the shaping of anti-Jewish attitudes of societies and the policies of governments. The most devastating lethal metastasis of this process occurred in our own century during the Holocaust. Faced with this history from which we as Christians cannot, and must not, dissociate ourselves, we ask God's forgiveness through our Lord Jesus Christ. We pray for divine grace that will enable us, more

firmly than ever before, to turn from this path of rejection and persecution to affirm that Judaism has not been superseded by Christianity; that Christianity is not to be understood as the successor religion to Judaism; God's covenant with the Jewish people has not been abrogated. God has not rejected the Jewish people; God is faithful in keeping covenant.[27]

In 1990 came "A Message to the Churches" from the United Church of Christ's Theological Panel on Jewish-Christian Relations. The statement was clear on the continuing vitality of Judaism and in its flat rejection of the view that Christianity had replaced or "superseded" it.

We affirm with the apostle [Paul] that God has not abrogated their covenant. Such an irrevocable call, with its supporting gifts, contradicts the supersessionist view that God has rescinded the covenant with Israel. We believe that to deny God's irrevocable covenant with the chosen people has led and continues to lead to the "teaching of contempt" for Jews, with its horrifying results. We reject that view.[28]

This affirmation raised a fundamental question: If Judaism remained in covenant with God even after Jesus, did this mean that there was salvation outside the church? Did it mean that Christians reached God through Jesus, but that Jews could reach Him without Jesus, by being true to their own faith? The United Church of Christ grappled with the issue and could not reach a conclusion: "We have examined a number of ways of interpreting this double affirmation, and are drawn to some and reject others. Our affirmation both of the continuing covenant of God with the Jewish people and of fulfillment of God's promises in Christ appears to be a paradox."[29]

The Presbyterian Church, too, issued a "study document" called "A Theological Understanding of the Relationship Between Christians and Jews," approved by its 199th General Assembly in 1987.

The statement offered a clear and emotional rejection of anti-Semitism, recognizing the role of Christians and Christian teaching in propagating it in the past.

> We acknowledge in repentance the church's long and deep complicity in the proliferation of anti-Jewish attitudes and actions through its "teaching of contempt" for the Jews. Such teaching we now repudiate, together with the acts and attitudes which it generates. . . .
>
> To this day, the church's worship, preaching, and teaching often lend themselves, at times unwittingly, to a perpetuation of the "teaching of contempt." For example, the public reading of Scripture without explicating potentially misleading passages concerning "the Jews," preaching which uses Judaism as a negative example in order to commend Christianity, public prayer which assumed that only the prayers of Christians are pleasing to God, teaching in the church school which reiterates stereotypes and nonhistorical ideas about the Pharisees and Jewish leadership—all of these contribute, however subtly, to a continuation to the church's "teaching of contempt."[30]

It continued with a somber reflection on the Holocaust, and promised that Presbyterians would never permit the church's past behavior to be repeated:

> It is agonizing to discover that the church's "teaching of contempt" was a major ingredient that made possible the monstrous policy of annihilation of Jews by Nazi Germany. It is disturbing to have to admit that the churches of the West did little to challenge the policies of their governments, even in the face of growing certainty that the Holocaust was taking place. . . . As the very embodiment of anti-Jewish attitudes and actions, the Holocaust is a sober reminder that such horrors are actually possible in this world, and that they begin with apparently small acts of disdain or expedience. Hence we pledge to be alert for all such acts of denigration from now on, so that they may be resisted. We also pledge

resistance to any such actions, perpetrated by anyone, anywhere. . . . We must be willing to admit our church's complicity in wrongdoing in the past, even as we try to establish a new basis of trust and communication with Jews. We pledge, God helping us, never again to participate in, to contribute to, or to allow the persecution or denigration of Jews or the belittling of Judaism.[31]

The document was also clear in its rejection of supersessionism, the notion that Christianity has replaced Judaism:

The long and dolorous history of Christian imperialism, in which the church has often justified anti-Jewish acts and attitudes in the name of Jesus, finds its theological base in this teaching. We believe and testify that this teaching of supersessionism is harmful and in need of reconsideration. . . . For us, the teaching that the church has been engrafted by God's grace into the people of God finds as much support in Scripture as supersessionism, and is much more consistent with our Reformed understanding of the work of God in Jesus Christ. . . . God's covenants are not broken. . . . The church has not 'replaced' the Jewish people.[32]

Here again the question arose as to whether there is a kind of dual covenant. The Presbyterians stated that "We affirm that the reign of God is attested by the continuing existence of the Jewish people. . . . Hence, when speaking with Jews about matters of faith, we must always acknowledge that Jews are already in covenantal relationship with God." But the matter was a very difficult one: "For Christians, there is no easy answer to this matter. . . . In light of Scripture which testifies to God's repeated offer of forgiveness to Israel, we do not presume to judge in God's place."[33]

What the United Church of Christ called a "paradox" the Presbyterians called a "mystery."

The continued existence of the Jewish people and of the church as communities elected by God is, as the Apostle Paul expressed it, a "mystery." We do not claim to fathom this mystery, but we cannot ignore it. At the same time we cannot forget that we stand in a covenant established by Jesus Christ and that faithfulness to that covenant requires us to call all women and men to faith in Jesus Christ.[34]

Finally, this brief survey of mainline Protestant attitudes toward Judaism must include the 1993 "Statement on Relations Between Jews and Christians" of the Christian Church/Disciples of Christ. The statement was very clear on past Christian anti-Semitism, noting that "Each of Hitler's laws found its precedent in a law passed by councils of the church." "We confess and repent," it continued, "of the church's long and deep collusion in the spread of anti-Jewish attitudes and action through its 'teaching of contempt' for Jews and Judaism." It discussed New Testament references to the Jews as well: "Christians must acknowledge that the language of invective, condemnation, and rejection, vexing and difficult as it is to understand, is present in the New Testament and throughout most of the traditions of the church. This language has all too often gone hand in hand with actions undertaken by Christians against Jews."

The statement took up the issue of Judaism today, maintaining that "the covenant established by God's grace with the Jewish people has not been abrogated but remains valid." What would this mean for evangelism of the Jews?

Although we do not want to say Judaism is for Jews and the church for Gentiles, we must acknowledge that the continued existence of the Jewish people who do not confess the lordship of Jesus Christ and who see their Jewishness as incompatible with this confession is, as Paul the apostle declares, a mystery.

The statement then discussed what must be done to counteract this history of anti-Semitism, declaring it "necessary to declare . . . [that] anti-Jewish teaching and practices by Christians must be stopped and eradicated." As to practical steps, "Study of Jewish history and thought should not stop with the first century. All Christians need to have some introduction of the great rabbinical heritage, to Jewish history and religion up to the present time, and to the story of Christian persecution of the Jews."[35]

Examples of Protestant statements on Jews and Judaism could fill up volumes. Those few given here show how very far many churches have now gone. They have admitted the role of Christianity in spreading anti-Semitic beliefs and accepted responsibility for the church's part in the bloody history of anti-Semitism. And they have undertaken a new evaluation of Judaism's ongoing vitality. Most accept, or at least cannot deny, that a covenant still exists under which the Jews have their own continuing relationship with God.

Have the impressive statements quoted here actually filtered down to individual churches and their teachings? One way of judging is by looking at Sunday school and other church textbooks. Philip Cunningham's study of Catholic texts has its counterpart in Stuart Polly's 1992 work, *The Portrayal of Jews and Judaism in Current Protestant Teaching Materials*.[36] Polly reviewed two mainline groups, the United Methodist Church and the Presbyterians. His conclusions were mixed.

A Methodist teacher's guide, for example, contained this excellent statement on the crucifixion:

> Obviously only a few of the Jewish leaders had a hand in Jesus' death. . . . Further, in every way, the Romans were equally implicated at every stage.
>
> . . . crucifixion was a form of capital punishment that the Romans used for enemies of the state. . . .

This text [Matt 27:1-2) contains much strong language against the Jewish people and blames them for the death of Jesus. We should remember that the crowd at the trial did not represent the whole Jewish nation. Only the religious leaders were present. In fact, some scholars speculate that . . . the Pharisees, who might have been more friendly to Jesus, were not even informed about the trial. Further, Jesus' disciples were also Jews. Even if the Jewish people of Jesus' time did not accept him, that is certainly no reason to blame Jews born later. It should not be used as an excuse to perpetuate hostility. . . . It would be more accurate to say that Jesus was killed by his contemporaries.[37]

On the other hand, the student lesson didn't include this material, leaving open the possibility that the teacher would never convey one whit of it to the students.

Methodist texts varied on the subject of Judaism, but Polly quoted one that contained a very positive statement: "We sometimes forget that, until near the end of the first century, Christianity was a Jewish sect. . . . Christianity does not abandon Judaism but grows out of it. There is continuity rather than discontinuity. This is the real meaning of fulfillment. And this continuity can be a basis for mutual respect."[38] The Methodist texts, Polly found, contained the best statements reminding students that Jesus was a Jew, and handled the crucifixion very well. While Jews would not accept many of the statements implying that divine grace is available only through Jesus, Methodist texts had clearly been revised to exclude many of the old prejudices about Jews and Judaism, particularly those connected to the crucifixion.

Presbyterian texts were given a similar, moderately positive review. Polly quoted one student exercise dealing with the Crucifixion: "News Release, April A.D. 30. Three criminals were executed this afternoon by Roman authorities. One of the three was a Jewish rabbi who taught about the coming kingdom of God."[39] This statement blames the Romans entirely, not the Jews, for the death of Jesus—and clearly identified Jesus to the student as a Jew. Another statement made a very positive reference to contemporary Judaism: "What do young people know about the importance of Passover to the history of the people of Israel? They know about it as an event in the distant history of the Israelites in Egypt. Do they know that it is celebrated and remembered every year in Jewish homes?"[40] Polly found numerous positive references to present-day Judaism in the Presbyterian materials. On the other hand, there was in all the materials Polly reviewed only one reference to the Holocaust, and that one made no reference to Jews as its target.

This was a recurrent theme: few Protestant educational materials covered the Holocaust at all, or at all well, from the Jewish perspective. Indeed, there was little apparent effort to carry through into school texts that portion of official church statements dealing with the history of Christian anti-Semitism. Still, anti-Semitic material per se, and especially the deicide accusation, had been carefully excluded from most texts.

Polly concluded that perhaps the largest problem in most Protestant texts was the silence with respect to modern Judaism.

> The high frequency of references to Jews and Judaism in biblical times is matched by a near silence regarding Judaism since the first century. . . . As a result, two thousand years of the development of rabbinic Judaism . . . are ignored. Curriculum editors and writers seem to have no problem with this gap in Jewish history. . . . Judaism as a living religion is not discussed in these curricula. . . . there is a theological underpinning to this pedagogy which often claims that Christianity replaced Judaism as the path to God. The result is a studied avoidance of Judaism as a living faith.[41]

It is taking Protestant groups longer to come to grips with the presentation of Jews and Judaism in textbooks than it has taken the Roman Catholic Church. For one thing, Roman Catholics have a more centralized governing structure that permits decisions to percolate down faster. But more important, the Roman Catholic Church has gone much further in its rethinking of Judaism. Still, for the mainline Protestant denominations, there is at least a beginning. Official church statements on Jews and Judaism have changed profoundly, and textbooks are starting to follow. These reflect some reassessment, such as that with respect to Jesus' death and his identity as a Jew, but they still have far to go, especially in the areas of post-Biblical and modern Judaism and Jewish history. This is an area of great opportunity for interfaith dialogue, for it is one of great interest to Christians and Jews where discussions can likely lead to real additional progress.

The Question of Proselytization

For most Christian denominations, as words like "mystery" and "paradox" show, assessing the relationship between God and the Jews today, after the life of Jesus, is an enormously complex theological endeavor. It brings into question some of the most fundamental Christian beliefs about salvation, Jesus' role, and the nature of God's relations with non-Christians in general and Jews in particular. Some denominations have adopted a "dual covenant" approach, but this raises yet another great issue for them: should there be no proselytizing among Jews? Are Jews exempt from the otherwise universal call, the "Great Commission," for "witnessing" and for evangelization? For historical reasons, perhaps, the West German bishops of the Protestant Evangelical Synod of the Rhineland went furthest in this direction, stating in 1980 that

> We believe that in their respective calling Jews and Christians are witnesses to God before the world and before each other. Therefore we are

convinced that the church may not express its witness towards the Jewish people as it does its mission to the peoples of the world.[42]

But the clarity of this view is rare, and the matter of "mission" remains a difficult one for Christians theologically—and for Jews who are assessing contemporary Christian attitudes. What is it fair for Jews to expect? Rabbi David Novak, professor of Jewish Studies at the University of Toronto, has said that it is "unreasonable for Jews to expect Christians to cease proclaiming the Gospel [and] un-Christian for Christians themselves to abandon their obligation to proclaim the gospel irrespective of how lofty the motive, even for the sake of reconciliation with the Jews." But he has drawn a line:

> dialogue between Jews and Christians is virtually impossible with those Christian groups who insist on maintaining specific "missions to the Jews." For these missions, traditionally, have been used as centers to lure Jews away from their heritage, from their own unique covenant with God. Missions to the Jews have been feared by Jews as preying upon the most physically and emotionally desperate, and the most spiritually immature members of our people. Moreover, out of these specific missionary efforts, especially, have come a virulent type of denigration of Judaism as either warped, blind, or primitive.[43]

That is the proper line to draw. It is unreasonable for Jews to demand of Christians that they abandon a central tenet of their faith, which calls for evangelizing—for spreading the Gospel to the world. Indeed, from the Jewish perspective, Christian evangelizing has brought knowledge of the Hebrew Bible and of the Ten Commandments to millions never reached by Judaism. But the rejection of Jews and Judaism that usually accompanied efforts to spread the Gospel has meant disaster for the Jews.[44] If, today, Christian churches have abandoned their traditional contempt for Judaism, perhaps the wish to spread the Gospel will not be attended in the future by episodes of anti-Semitic talk and activities. Evangelical activities are not inherently anti-Semitic, any more than Jewish efforts to convert Christians are inherently the mark of bigotry or a deprecation of Christianity. What determines whether evangelizing is anti-Semitic is what is underlying it—and Christian attitudes toward Judaism have changed enormously in the last few decades.

But these new attitudes are incompatible with targeting Jews for special evangelical efforts. Rabbi Novak provides a useful rule of thumb. Christian activities that seek to spread Christian beliefs are not inherently anti-Semitic, but those that focus specifically—and exclusively—on Jews immediately raise a red flag. With this in mind, the evangelical activities of the Roman Catholic Church and of most mainline Protestant denominations cannot be called anti-Semitic in motive, form, or effect.

The State of Israel

Where Catholics and mainline Protestants still fall short is in their failure to understand the relationship of most Jews to Israel.

Typical is the United Church of Christ's 1990 statement that, though deeply repentant for past sins against Jews, was remarkably ungenerous when it came to Israel:

> We do not see consensus in the United Church of Christ or among our panel on the covenantal significance of the state of Israel. We appreciate the compelling moral argument for the creation of modern Israel as a vehicle for self-determination and as a haven for a victimized people; we also recognize that this event has entailed the dispossession of Palestinians from their homes and the denial of human rights.[45]

Indeed at some points the statement referred to "the State of Israel-Palestine" and used the term "Uprising" to refer to Arab activities most Israelis see as terrorist violence against them.[46]

This was at best a dry evenhandedness and conveyed no sense of joy at contemplating Israel restored. The Lutherans spoke in a similar vein: "It seems clear that there is no consensus among Lutherans with respect to the relation between the 'chosen people' and the territory comprising the present State of Israel."[47] Presbyterians endorsed Palestinian statehood, "stand in solidarity with Palestinians as they cry for justice as the dispossessed," and were careful to distinguish themselves from Christian Zionists who see religious significance in the re-establishment of the state of Israel.[48] In fact, one can search very long among mainline Protestants statements to find a sympathetic word about Israel.

Rabbi Mordecai Waxman summed up the problem:

> From the Jewish point of view . . . a central reality of contemporary Jewish existence has not been properly dealt with by the Christian churches. The existence, significance, and meaning of the State of Israel to the Jewish people cannot be overestimated. In the Jewish theological and religious assessment the State represents a fulfillment of Jewish history, a validation of the ongoing covenant, and the major creative response to the Holocaust. . . . Jews . . . see its existence as the beginning of a great overturn in Jewish history and as the opening to new developments in sacred history. Christians apparently cannot share this vision nor the psychology and history which have created it.[49]

If this is not, in itself, a form of anti-Semitism, it nevertheless explains a great deal about the lack of sympathy American Jews feel toward American Christianity. For millions of Jews, Israel is a tremendously emotional matter, and in many cases a source of their Jewish identity. It is very difficult to credit as sympathetic to Jews and Judaism those who are totally unsympathetic to Israel. This is not a matter of theology. Few Jews know or care much about where Israel fits in the theology of mainline Protestantism. What they *do* know is that among the mainline Protestant denominations there is a lack of will to understand what Israel means to American Jews.

The effect of this is an emotional estrangement, a feeling on the part of Jews of distance, even hostility, to Christians. In fact, mainline attitudes toward Israel (which have occasionally included vociferous criticism of Israeli behavior and support for the PLO) are probably much better known to American Jews than church policy statements about Judaism. Similarly, the numerous Catholic statements are little known, while the church's past refusal to grant diplomatic recognition to Israel is widely recognized. Thus, the churches get little credit from Jews for what they do right, and are better known for what they do—or did—wrong.

The immense changes in Christian attitudes toward Jews and Judaism have been amazingly underreported and underappreciated in the American Jewish community. In most Christian denominations, a two-thousand-year-old war against Judaism is being called off and its direct connection to anti-Semitic violence admitted. Contemptuous and hostile attitudes toward Judaism that date back to the years immediately after Jesus' death have been questioned, criticized, rejected. The historic role of Judaism has been appreciated and reaffirmed, and in many cases its ongoing covenant with God has been acknowledged. Efforts to convert Jews to Christianity have been questioned in some churches and brought under strict controls in others. This is revolutionary.

And as it helps explain the falling levels of anti-Semitism in the United States, so it suggests why those levels will continue to fall. This will be so especially if Protestants follow Catholics in ensuring that church texts used in teaching children, and in preaching, reflect these new understandings of Judaism.

These changes should give rise to new Jewish attitudes toward Christians and toward Christian religiosity. But in recent years,

Jewish fears have not diminished; instead they have been more narrowly targeted toward the "Christian right"—politically conservative Christians associated with evangelical churches. It is to those groups, and their views of Jews and Judaism, that we now turn. Whatever the progress among Catholics and mainline Protestants, are the "evangelicals" now the carriers of anti-Semitic attitudes? Does their growing strength threaten Jewish interests, and does it justify continuing Jewish resistance to enhancing religion's role in American life?

Chapter 4

EVANGELICALS

JEWISH FEARS of religion in America are aroused by the idea of what a more vigorous Christianity might mean in our society. As has been noted, Jews have responded with anxiety to the recent rise of what is variously called the "Christian right," the "evangelicals," or Christian conservatives. Today, evangelical Christians and the Jewish community are on a collision course. In the current war over religion and secularism, the evangelicals, or Christian Right, are on one side of the barricade and most Jews are on the other.

Many Jews associate conservative Christians with anti-Semitism, for political as well as religious reasons. According to a 1994 survey done for the American Jewish Committee, "American Jews . . . tend to suspect even the nonextremist right of anti-Jewish prejudice. Jews perceive Republicans and conservatives as more anti-Semitic than Democrats and liberals."[1] Thus the suspicions founded in religion are increased by those that Jews hold of the political right, and by now the precise admixture of the two is difficult to measure.

Nor does conservative Christian support for Israel much affect this perception. Many Jews discount that support as motivated by Christian theological interpretations that see the creation of the state of Israel and the settlement of Jews there as part of a New Testament prophecy about the Second Coming of Jesus. They find the theology offensive, and the support for Israel—motivated "only" by Christianity—unreliable.

Fear of the Christian right often leads Jewish spokesmen to vilify it. Harvard Law School Professor Alan Dershowitz entered the fray with his assertions (in his best-seller, *Chutzpah*) that "there can be no doubt that an explicit campaign is under way, by the Christian right, to establish Christianity as the official religion of America" and to "convert Jews or, at the very least, to relegate them to second-class status in their Christian America."[2] Rabbi Alexander Schindler, the longtime leader of American Reform Judaism, claimed in 1980 that "right wing Christian fundamentalism has been accompanied by the most serious outbreak of anti-Semitism in America since the end of World War II"[3] and warned American Jews that the Moral Majority was "a threat to American democracy [and] to America's Jews."[4]

The typical Jewish view of evangelicals—not universal, but certainly dominant—is grim indeed. One evangelical described it memorably:

> To most Jews, evangelicals are "New Religious Right" fundamentalists who endanger free thought and social progress. Their world view contributes to anti-Semitism and anti-intellectualism. Their representatives include leaders who declare "God Almighty does not hear the prayer of a Jew;" little children who insist on screaming Bible verses outside a public school; missionaries who hawk gospel tracts on street corners to seduce Jewish young people to "accept Jesus as their Savior"; beauty queens in low-cut bathing suits who smile sweetly as they tell how much they "love Jesus;" and personalities like Jerry Falwell, Jim and Tammy Bakker, Jimmy Swaggert, and even Billy Graham.[5]

The late Nathan Perlmutter, for many years national director of the Anti-Defamation League, once wrote, quite similarly, that "our image of the Fundamentalist and the Evangelical is a kind of collage assembled out of bits and pieces from Theodore Dreiser, Sinclair Lewis, and Erskine Caldwell. . . . Even after all this time, memories of that great swarm of sex-ridden, Bible-thumping caricatures continue to exert a pervasive power."[6] Most American Jews were "turned off" by revivalism as a matter of cultural style and frightened by the presumed (and all too frequently present) anti-Semitism and the "convert the Jews" missionary work that too often accompanied it.

Such characterizations find an eager audience among the Jews, in part because the Jewish community and evangelical Christians do not know each other very well. The Anti-Defamation League has referred to a "virtual absence of interaction between Jewish and evangelical groups."[7] Until very recent years, the concentration of Jews in several large, mostly Eastern cities and the concentration of evangelicals outside of those cities meant that physical, and social, contacts were limited. Even today, when interfaith activities between Jews and the Roman Catholic Church or the mainline Protestant denominations are frequent, they are rare between Jewish groups and evangelicals. Thus the unrelievedly negative Jewish view of evangelicals is unlikely to change quickly.

But with the hostility, there is much confusion. Are all conservative Christians evangelicals? Are all evangelicals conservatives? The National Association of Evangelicals is not a political group and is not to be compared to the Christian Coalition—a political organization whose members are likely to be—though not always—evangelical Protestants. Such distinctions abound, but for the majority of American Jews they are out of reach.

Of course, the misunderstandings go both ways. Many evangelicals know relatively little about Jews, though they know much more about Judaism. They take their knowledge from the church, from Sunday school classes, and from reading the Bible. Thus they tend to see Judaism as the religion of the Hebrew Bible, and to know almost nothing about post-biblical developments. Often "Jews are portrayed as wealthy and talented, blessed by God,"[8] even though they reject Jesus; indeed, philo-Semitism has a long history among evangelicals: "The early fundamentalist-evangelical movement believed that God was pro-Jewish and that those who hurt the Jewish people would be punished directly by God."[9]

Part of the problem is that evangelicals speak a language, saturated both with public assertions of religiosity and with Christian references, that is foreign to most Jews. For example, many Sunday school texts urge children to be selective in their choice of friends, and warn against intimate social interaction with people who are not true Christians.[10] Such warnings may seem to warn against friendship with Jews, but in fact, given the few Jews and many nonevangelical Christians with whom young evangelicals come into contact, they are not aimed at Jews at all. They are primarily efforts to combat cultural trends that lead to sexual activity and teen pregnancy, by urging evangelical youth to date others who share their values. It would be ironic for Jews to campaign, on the one hand, for their own children to limit dating with Christians and not to marry Christians, but to call it anti-Semitism if evangelicals seek essentially the same result!

Is the Christian Right Anti-Semitic?

Despite the perception among Jews that Christian religiosity and fundamentalist religious beliefs are strongly linked to anti-Semitism, the relationship is extremely weak or altogether nonexistent. "Among non-Jews, fundamentalism does not promote anti-Semitic attitudes," a 1991 American Jewish Committee study found.[11] A 1992 Anti-Defamation League report came to the same conclusion:

[R]eligious beliefs appear to have little impact one way or the other on anti-Semitism. . . .There is little difference in levels of anti-Semitic propensity among the principal religious denominations in the U.S. The relative importance of religion in an individual's life does not appear to be linked with anti-Jewish prejudice. Christian fundamentalists are not significantly more likely to accept anti-Semitic attitudes than other Americans.[12]

In addition, contrary to the image of devout Christians cherished by many Jews, evangelicals are equally split between Democrats and Republicans* and have educational backgrounds roughly the same as those of other Americans.[13]

And evangelicals are strongly pro-Israel. In fact, "after American Jews, the strongest supporters of Israel in the United States are white evangelical Protestants."[14] Roughly a quarter million of them visit Israel every year, meaning that most American visitors to Israel are Christian, not Jewish. Jews tend to be suspicious of evangelical enthusiasm for Israel, seeing it as motivated by evangelical religious

---

*Jews believe that political conservatism is linked to anti-Semitism, but the evidence contradicts this prejudice. A 1994 survey for the American Jewish Committee put it squarely:

> American Jews . . . tend to suspect even the nonextremist right of anti-Jewish prejudice. Jews perceive Republicans and conservatives as more anti-Semitic than Democrats and liberals. However, while anti-Semitism is clearly associated with right-wing extremism both historically and currently, there is little connection between anti-Semitism and nonextremist political or partisan orientation. . . . those studies that have investigated the political correlates find little association with self-identified political ideology, presidential vote, or partisan preference. [Tom W. Smith, *Anti-Semitism in Contemporary America* (New York: American Jewish Committee, 1994), pp. 25–26.]

Similarly, a 1991 survey for the AJC concluded that "Party identification has little relationship with attitudes about Jews. . . . there is thus little support for the idea that conservatives or right-wingers are especially anti-Semitic. There appears to be little ideological/partisan basis for contemporary anti-Semitism." [Tom W. Smith, *What Do Americans Think About Jews* (New York: American Jewish Committee, 1991), p. 23.]

views. Yet the support of most Jews for Israel is based, even if indirectly, on their religious affiliation; why can Christians not, with equal legitimacy, have the same motivation? Many Jews argue that evangelicals favor Jewish control of the Holy Land because they see it as a step toward the messianic era when Jesus returns, and therefore as a means to an end inimical to Judaism. But the support itself is surely no less valuable or authentic. Even those (indeed, perhaps especially those) who do not expect the return of Jesus promised in the New Testament must see that Christian support for Israel is founded in a belief that guarantees continuing dedication to Israel's well-being.

In fact, Christian Zionism is a very old movement, not a recent manifestation of evangelical fervor. As early as 1878, evangelical leaders such as William Blackstone were writing about building a Jewish homeland in Palestine. The "Blackstone Memorial" of 1891 was a declaration urging the U.S. government to back this step—more than two decades before the Balfour Declaration and six years before Theodore Herzl's first Zionist Congress in Switzerland in 1897.

When in 1917 the British government issued the Balfour Declaration, promising "a national home for the Jewish people" in Palestine, mainline Christian denominations were hostile, while evangelicals were enthusiastic. They have maintained that enthusiasm to this day, while many mainline denominations, as well as the National Council of Churches and the World Council of Churches, have been consistently hostile to Israel and friendly to its critics and its enemies. When a group of mainline Christian organizations publicly attacked the Clinton administration in early 1995 for "failing to recognize . . . Palestinian rights in Jerusalem" and called for a redivision of the city, the so-called Christian right rushed to Israel's defense. In a letter to congressional leaders dated March 14, 1995, the Christian Coalition reasserted its support for Israel, rejected the criticism, and called for moving the U.S. embassy in Israel to Jerusalem, which, it said, must remain the undivided capital of Israel. Meanwhile, in a feat of perfect timing, the National Council of Jewish Women issued a memo on March 14, 1995, announing the schedule for its forthcoming "Institute" in Washington. The Washington conference would begin, the memo said, with a "Keynote Address" from the Rev. Barry Lynn. Rev. Lynn, a well-known liberal spokesman and executive director of Americans United for Separation of Church and State, would be entitling his address "Radical Right: Radically Wrong!"

Moreover, it is well worth noting that Zionism aside, evangelicals were far more concerned about reports of growing anti-Semitic violence in Germany in the 1930s than the mainline denominations. "The movement on the whole recognized at an early date that the Holocaust was impending and believed that six million Jews had been murdered at a time when more liberal Christians were labeling this Jewish 'atrocity propaganda.'"[15]

The point is, as the ability and willingness of American Jews to promote pro-Israel policies erode, support from evangelical groups that are growing in size and political influence should be viewed with gratitude, not suspicion, by Americans who are concerned about Israel's future. When the "Israel Lobby" in Washington consists not only of Jews but of leading evangelical Christian organizations, it becomes much stronger.

Prejudice and Politics

Still, American Jews are on the whole uncomfortable among Christian activists for two reasons, neither of which does them credit. The first is simple prejudice: suspicion of Christian religiosity that has little or nothing to do, today, with actual manifestations of anti-Semitism by devout Christians. Jews who believe that evangelical

Christians are likely to be anti-Semites, and that Christian religiosity is associated with anti-Semitism, are indulging in prejudice in the dictionary definition of the term. They are prejudging their fellow citizens and condemning them for bigotry without evidence and without trial. This attitude might once have been understandable in view of the long history of Christian anti-Semitism, but it is indefensible in America today. Bias against black or Hispanic citizens is automatically and roundly condemned in the Jewish community as plain bigotry, and so it should be. It seems to be another matter when the target is religious Christians. Anti-Christian bias is apparently the only form of prejudice that remains respectable in the American Jewish community. This should be anathema to American Jews—not only because it may embitter interfaith relations but because it is entirely contrary to the respect for religious differences for which Jews have clamored over the years.

For decades, leaders of mainline Christian denominations and of the National Council of Churches who were unvaryingly hostile to Israel were viewed as appropriate partners for the Jewish community in interfaith dialogues and political endeavors. They were never subject to the kind of attacks launched against Christian conservatives—because they were graduates of the finest seminaries and were men and women of social prestige, and because they were people of liberal political bent.

Such a stance is dishonorable for the American Jewish community and does nothing to advance its real interests. The notion that the more fervent a Christian's belief the more danger he or she represents to Jews should be rejected outright. The view that Christians who oppose current court readings of the religion clauses of the First Amendment are probably dangerous anti-Semites deserves rejection as well. Such attitudes insult, and alienate, many devout Christians who are allies not only when it comes to the security of Israel but in the struggle against bigotry in America as well.

Indeed, so foreign to Jewish tradition and Jewish interests is this prejudice against people who devoutly practice another religion that one must seek an additional explanation for it, beyond prejudice founded on a powerful, historical fear of a vibrant Christianity. And the second answer is *politics*. Many Jews dislike the so-called Christian right as much for being "right" as for being Christian. In a statement reacting to criticism of the Rev. Pat Robertson, for example, Hyman Bookbinder, the longtime Washington director of the American Jewish Committee, admitted that Robertson "is one of the most eloquent defenders of Israel," but he added that "we cannot let that blind us to the need for a Jewish program for social justice."[16]

Bookbinder was at least absolutely open: evangelicals may support Israel, but that pales in comparison with the importance of the liberal political agenda. So many Jews and Jewish organizations define Jewish interests as identical to that agenda that they reflexively see conservative Christians as powerful opponents. What is more, after disingenuously and dangerously misrepresenting their own views as "Jewish" rather than as "liberal," they then imply that opposing views are not only conservative but also "anti-Jewish."

Moreover, Jews who now complain about the role of Christian activists in public life, or about religion in politics, were silent about these "problems" when they agreed with the political goals being put forward. When black preachers led the civil rights movement and black churches were at its heart, Jews marched alongside those preachers—and did not complain that they were "injecting religion into politics." In fact, wrote Stephen Carter, "There is little about the civil rights movement that makes it very different from the right-wing religious movements of the present day" in this respect.[17] No major Jewish group complained when Martin Luther King publicly denounced the Vietnam War. When Catholic bishops in the 1980s felt compelled to promote a nuclear freeze, a popular liberal cause in those days, the major Jewish groups did not protest.

All too many Jewish leaders consider religion a legitimate, even laudable motivation for Jewish activists or Christian clergy when they are promoting the liberal agenda. But when it comes to conservative Christians the rules change, and suddenly representatives of the major Jewish organizations are warning the nation that it faces a dangerous intrusion of religion into political life.

The Anti-Defamation League's 1994 attack on Christian conservatives, *The Religious Right: The Assault on Tolerance and Pluralism in America,* ignored these distinctions and reasserted the faulty argument that those who do not share the liberal political agenda and the traditional, fearful liberal view of religion are a danger to American Jews. The ADL text stated that "hostility to the Constitution's separation of church and state is the defining feature of religious right groups and activists,"[18] and that "hostility" was seen as a sure sign of anti-Jewish prejudice.

The ADL rhetoric was powerful. The report denounced the religious right's "hostility to tolerance and pluralism," its "hostility to difference," even its "basic rejection of the modern democratic state." ADL National Director Abe Foxman's press release about the report warned of the religious right's "rhetoric of fear, suspicion, and even hatred that strains the democratic process." Christian conservatives were referred to as "prophets of rage" guilty of "paranoia and scapegoating" who associate with "homophobes, conspiracists, and concerted foes of church and state separation."[19]

But the report intended to document his charges is a sloppy piece of work: over 150 pages of text but no source notes, and so error-ridden that the ADL was forced to issue a number of corrections and apologies in letters and memos. Given the enormous sensitivity of the subject matter—an attack on some famous Americans, including valuable supporters of Israel—this alone is a remarkable

fact. Among the more egregious examples: After the report casti-
gated the Rev. Pat Robertson for failing to denounce the Louisiana
neo-Nazi David Duke, Director Abe Foxman had to write to
Robertson to apologize, admitting that "you did denounce Duke
on your 700 Club broadcast . . . three days before the election."
Moreover, the report carried the very unsettling news that "at a
1980 CBN [Christian Broadcasting Network] staff prayer meeting,
Robertson stated that Jews were spiritually deaf and spiritually
blind." But Foxman acknowledged in his letter of apology that "We
have discovered that you did not make these statements at this
meeting."[20] It is noteworthy that the ADL was not able to make
this "discovery" before publishing its report.

The report's definition of its subject matter is just as interesting.
The "religious right," it says, is "an array of politically conservative
groups and individuals who are attempting to influence public
policy based on a shared cultural philosophy that is antagonistic to
pluralism and church/state separation."[21] Attempting to influence
public policy is beyond criticism, one assumes, for Jewish groups
such as the ADL; and the "cultural philosophy" in question has
a great deal in common with that propounded by Orthodox Jews
(on issues such as homosexuality, abortion, and sex education in
schools) and by politically conservative Jews (on issues such as
crime and welfare reform). The gravamen of the charge against the
Christian groups, then, is in their alleged opposition to pluralism
and church/state separation.

And what is the evidence that they are "antagonistic to pluralism
and church/state separation?" The ADL report takes a tripartite
approach to the question. In the first place it employs the distasteful tactic of guilt by association to link Christian conservatives to
fringe groups and extreme opinions. One man writes an article for
a magazine where years earlier someone else who is an extremist
wrote an article, revealing . . . what? Second, it provides inaccurate

information about other Christian conservatives, so as to make them appear extreme—or more extreme than they would otherwise seem, as it did in the case of Pat Robertson. Third, it defines pluralism as requiring adherence to liberal politics and calls opposing views "intolerant." The report notes that conservative Christians oppose "gay rights," seek limits on abortion, and support school prayer, and states that "hostility to the Constitution's separation of church and state is the defining feature of religious right groups and activists."[22] It is as if no disagreement on this issue were possible, making an anti-Semite of any law professor who thinks some Supreme Court interpretations of the Constitution are far-fetched— and of any justice who files a dissenting opinion. The ADL report claims that "nothing more aptly characterizes the religious right movement than its hostility to difference, both within its own faith tradition and outside of it."[23] This criticism appears in a report that rejects "difference" on church-state issues as tantamount to bigotry!

The ADL report did real harm. It derailed a promising ADL effort to work with evangelicals on issues related to anti-Semitism. Not surprisingly, the evangelicals felt wronged by the report and withdrew from the program, at least temporarily. It was personally offensive to many people mentioned unfairly in it, who saw their years of work on behalf of Israel answered with this kick in the teeth. And worse, many Christian conservatives who have made exceptional efforts to drive any taint of anti-Semitism out of both American Christianity and American conservatism saw their efforts dismissed and themselves unjustly accused of anti-Semitism (as was, for example, conservative leader Paul Weyrich) and of bigotry. At bottom, the ADL report is itself an assault on pluralism, based as it is on the view that there are correct and incorrect positions on cultural/political questions—and that only the liberal positions are correct.

Sadly, this kind of broadside against conservative Christian groups is not limited to the ADL. In its brief (thirty-two page) 1995 Annual Report, for example, the American Jewish Committee dedicated most of a page to denouncing the Christian Coalition for its "reactionary agenda." The Coalition's proposed "Contract with America" is called a "radical" document that would end the separation of church and state, and readers are told of "Christians who view Ralph Reed's Coalition with alarm" and who say the Coalition's "interfaith goodwill is . . . suspect." Reed is, in fact, the only individual singled out for a negative reference in the entire report.

No doubt devout Christians are more conservative on a wide range of political and social issues than most American Jews are— *but so are many devout Jews.** The preference for a more liberal political agenda over the one embraced by most devout and observant Jews and most devout and observant Christians is perfectly proper, but it should not be dressed up as a concern for the future of American Jewry. It is politics, pure and simple, and there is nothing wrong with it *when it is called by its real name.* Liberals fight for liberal causes, and conservatives for their own. But it is wrong to decry—on grounds of separation of church and state—the intrusion of the Christian right into politics while the intrusions of the

---

*Many Orthodox Jews would fail this AJC test. The traditional Jewish position on abortion rights is not "abortion on demand" (nor is it to bar abortion; very briefly put, it allows abortion to save the life of the mother). The traditional Jewish view of homosexuality is made crystal clear in Leviticus, where it is called an "abomination." Most Jews clearly oppose prayer in schools, although there are more divisions on related issues such as a "moment of silence," or as to school vouchers. But the ADL report, and too many Jews, view arguments on separation of church and state not as political differences but as sure signs of anti-Jewish prejudice. This is not a new phenomenon, and Naomi Cohen noted in her book *Jews in Christian America* (p. 99) that after disputes decades ago "the fusion in Jewish minds between abuses of separation and other forms of prejudice left an enduring suspicion that antiseparationism was a hand-maiden of anti-Semitism." That approach excludes fair debate on these critical constitutional issues.

Christian left are accepted and indeed celebrated. This is hypocrisy, and it is likely to be understood and resented as such by Christian conservatives.

Exaggerating the extent of anti-Semitism, smearing Christian conservatives as anti-Semitic, and defining the spread of Christian evangelical activities as inevitably threatening to Jews are bad enough acts taken by themselves. But they have another negative effect: they draw attention away from *far more serious and legitimate* Jewish concerns about evangelicals. The first of these is missionary activities targeting Jews, and the second is evangelical teachings about Judaism.

Missionary Work

How serious or dangerous are Christian efforts to convert Jews? Are such missionary activities anti-Semitic?

There are, as the earlier discussion of Catholic and mainline Protestant attitudes suggested, numerous divisions among Christians on the issue of converting Jews. Some (especially German Protestant groups) have gone so far as to say that it should be stopped, because the "old covenant" remains in existence and Jews therefore have a relationship with God that does not require the intercession of Jesus. Others reject that view entirely, but suggest that all evangelizing of Jews or any other people must be conducted with due respect for the individuals' beliefs and their right to disagree.

Evangelicals too may be split on this as an abstract matter, but of course evangelism is the very heart of their faith. To be sure, it is more common for them to evangelize friends and neighbors, even family members, than outsiders. As a leader of the Southern Baptist Convention remarked, "I don't view most members of my own family as having had a conversion experience and being true Christians."

While one may be born a Jew or convert to Judaism, evangelicals note, "Evangelical Christianity teaches that one is never born a Christian, but rather one may *become* a Christian."[24] And indeed anyone may, whether born a Jew or a Gentile. Evangelicals have repeatedly taken the position that Jews, as much as any gentiles, are proper targets for conversion.

In 1977, a resolution entitled "To Share Gospel With Jews" was presented to the Lutheran Church-Missouri Synod at its 52nd Regular Convention.

> WHEREAS The Jews have sinned and come short of the glory of God as well as the Gentiles . . . and WHEREAS the Jews have been redeemed by Christ as well as the Gentiles . . . and WHEREAS Salvation for the Jews is by grace through faith in Christ as well as for Gentiles . . . and WHEREAS Our Savior commissioned us to baptize and to teach all things He has commanded to the Jews as well as to the Gentiles . . . We of the Lutheran Church-Missouri Synod have too often bypassed the Jews in evangelism visits and in the opening of new mission stations and . . . bypassing the Jewish people in missions and evangelism is one of the worst forms of lovelessness, discrimination, and anti-Semitism possible. . . . Resolved, That we repent of any anti-Semitic acts, statements, and attitudes of the past; That we repent of our past neglect in evangelizing Jews.[25]

The convention ultimately adopted a resolution, entitled "To Encourage Evangelism Among the Jews," aimed at putting these views into effect and directing the activities of the Committee on Witnessing to Jewish People:

> Resolved, That we direct the Board for Evangelism to give priority to materials and programs for witness to Jewish people; and . . . That we encourage especially those congregations located in or near Jewish communities to reach out to the Jews and share our faith that Jesus of Nazareth is the promised Messiah.[26]

Vernon Grounds, president emeritus of the Conservative Baptist Seminary in Denver, put the point even more starkly. While acknowledging that Protestants were divided on these issues, his view was that

> we evangelicals maintain that by the whole Christ-event Judaism qua religion has been superseded, its propaedeutic purpose accomplished. Since Messiah has come and offered his culminating sacrifice, there is, as we see it, no temple, no priesthood, no altar, no atonement, no forgiveness, no salvation, and no eternal hope in Judaism as a religion.[27]

And the 1989 "Willowbank Declaration on the Christian Gospel and the Jewish People" issued by the World Evangelical Fellowship put this as plainly as possible:

> As the supreme way of demonstrating love, we seek to encourage the Jewish people, along with all other peoples, to receive God's gift of life through Jesus the Messiah, and accordingly the growing number of Jewish Christians brings us great joy. . . . We reaffirm our commitment to the Jewish people and our desire to share the Gospel with them. . . .
>
> We deny that there is any truth in the widespread notion that evangelizing Jews is needless because they are already in covenant with God through Abraham and Moses and so are already saved despite their rejection of Jesus Christ as Lord and Saviour. . . .
>
> We deny that any non-Christian faith, as such, will mediate eternal life with God. . . .
>
> We affirm that failing to preach the Gospel to the Jewish people would be a form of anti-Semitism.[28]

Finally, in mid-1996 the Southern Baptist Convention reasserted in similar terms that its members had the responsibility to evangelize Jews. The convention's statement read, in part, as follows:

RESOLUTION ON JEWISH EVANGELISM: Whereas, Our evangelistic efforts have largely neglected the Jewish people . . . and Whereas, There has been an organized effort on the part of some either to deny that the Jewish people need to come to their Messiah, Jesus, to be saved; or to claim, for whatever reason, that Christians have neither right nor obligation to proclaim the gospel to the Jewish people . . . Be It Resolved . . . That we recommit ourselves to prayer, especially for the salvation of the Jewish people . . . and Be It Finally Resolved, That we direct our energies and resources toward the proclamation of the gospel to the Jewish people.

How are Jews to react to this? Should they view evangelism per se as anti-Semitic? No—no more than Jewish missionary activity, whose expansion was proposed several years ago by the leader of Reform Jewry, would necessarily be anti-Christian.[29] It is certainly not anti-Semitism as that scourge was traditionally defined. For the many Christians who believe that salvation is available only through Jesus, the effort to spread that view, and thereby to save souls, can hardly be called anti-Semitism (or, for that matter, anti-Islam, anti-Buddhism, or anti- anything else).

Evangelical activity in itself is an unobjectionable private action in a free society. When Christians proclaim their faith and seek to persuade others (including other Christians who have not shared a "rebirth" or "conversion" experience) to share it, they are acting properly within the bounds of their faith. Moreover, Jews have no right to demand that no one in this open society ever speak to them about Christianity. As Rabbi Yehiel Eckstein of the International Fellowship of Christians and Jews says, "Jews will have to acknowledge that in a democratic country such as America, people have the right to preach as they believe."[30]

But specifically targeting Jews for conversion is quite another thing. It bespeaks the traditional contempt for Judaism, suggesting that Jews among all peoples are especially lacking or sinful and therefore especially needful of a new religion. This is the view rejected by the Roman Catholic Church, which holds instead, as noted earlier, that "the temptation to create organizations of any kind, especially for education or social assistance, to 'convert' Jews, is to be rejected."[31] The various Societies for Promoting Christianity Among the Jews that existed in the nineteenth century were precisely such organizations. Every Jew finds such activities deeply offensive and not a little frightening. The Lutheran Church-Missouri Synod's "Committee on Witnessing to the Jewish People" (now renamed "Task Force on Witnessing to Jewish People") and its resolution giving "priority to materials and programs for witness to the Jewish people" arouses in Jews exactly these emotions, as did the 1996 statement by the Southern Baptist Convention.

Evangelical support for such groups as "Jews for Jesus"—which consist of Jewish converts to Christianity trying to convert other Jews—is extremely disturbing to the vast majority of Jews. Members of "Jews for Jesus" may be people of conscience and good will, but while Christians welcome them as converts, Jews view them as dangerous apostates and aggressive proselytizers, and wish to have absolutely nothing to do with them. All religions take a very dim view of apostasy, but Christians should have a particular sensitivity to the horror that it holds for Jews. Jews are members of a group that is small and getting smaller, that was reduced in size by one-third in the recent past by mass murder at the hands of some Christians while the vast majority of the rest watched without comment.

With this in mind, evangelicals should understand why Jews are repelled by the sentiments expressed in the following passage. It is from a text distributed by one of the most important evangelical publishers, David C. Cook:

The organization called Jews for Jesus was founded in the early seventies. . . . But Jews for Jesus have been around for almost two thousand years! That's because the first people to believe in Jesus were Jews. Perhaps you have a Jewish friend who doesn't know the Lord. . . . But just because most Jews don't believe in Jesus is no reason to assume your friend is not interested. Most Jewish people have just never considered Jesus because no one ever took the time to introduce them to the Messiah.[32]

Rabbi Eckstein, who works closely with evangelicals, has noted the various ruses "messianic Jews" have used to lure Jews away from their religion. Among the more devious is a TV show called *The Jewish Voice,* which turns out to be a Christian missionary program, and the advertising of religious services to be held in "synagogues" that are in reality Christian houses of worship dedicated to converting Jews.[33]

Christian evangelicals who persist in these activities—or fail to denounce them—poison relations between the Jewish and evangelical communities. To Jews, who after all have the right to define what is and is not compatible with Judaism, belief in Jesus is not compatible. "A Jew who believes in Jesus Christ spurns his faith [and] abandons his community. . . . It is conversion to Christianity, pure and simple," Rabbi Eckstein wrote.[34] "Are Jews not justified," he asked, "in distrusting even responsible Christians who lend such Hebrew Christian groups moral or financial support . . . ? More than constituting an imposing threat to Jewish life and survival, Hebrew Christians are the source of much of the Jewish distrust of evangelicals and the discord in their relations."[35]

Evangelism is central to Christianity and—when it eschews the targeting of Jews, and is done without disrespect for Judaism and without coercion of any sort—cannot properly be viewed as anti-

Semitic or otherwise objectionable in purpose or practice. The targeting of Jews by the Missouri Synod Lutherans in 1977 was apparently understood to have violated this norm, for one year after the resolutions quoted above were passed, new ones were added. In 1978 the Commission on Witnessing to the Jewish People spoke with greater understanding:

> We desire to be sensitive to the danger that witnessing to Jewish people can result in misunderstanding and potential nurturing of anti-Semitic attitudes. We plead for understanding that we are not singling out the Jewish people as a special target for our evangelistic endeavors. . . . that we are not mounting a campaign to convert the Jewish people with techniques of evangelism which involve manipulation, pressure, and disrespect of the individual. . . .
>
> We state our commitment that we do love the Jewish people, that we stand with them in opposing all forms of anti-Semitism and injustice, that we join them in humanitarian concerns, and will continue to love them even when they choose not to accept our witness.[36]

This showed that in truth evangelism can be compatible with respect for those listening to the message—and those rejecting the message. Nevertheless, it is not reassuring that at more recent Missouri Synod conventions, "an expanded emphasis in Jewish evangelism" has been agreed to by consensus.*

Vernon Grounds, whose tough language (he himself acknowl-

---

*As I was writing this book I spoke with officials of the Missouri Synod, in an effort to ensure that I had not overlooked material produced since I had begun my research. After some effort I was connected with the right man, who handled the Task Force on Witnessing to Jewish People. He happily agreed to send me the material I requested, but he also took my affirmation that I was a Jew as an invitation to proselytize me, rather than as a suggestion that he pay due respect to my religious beliefs. He actually tried to begin converting me right there on the telephone. The incident is emblematic of the problem: what he no doubt saw as an act of love I experienced as an incident that, while not without its comic aspect, was nevertheless distasteful.

edged that it was "harsh and grating") was noted above, has also recently urged greater care in the nature of evangelical activity. What is more, he has suggested that Christians have special responsibilities if they are going to evangelize Jews: "We have . . . an inescapable obligation to do whatever we can in order to clear away the misunderstandings and misinterpretation which have dyed the pages of history with Jewish blood."[37]

Indeed, he acknowledges the critical separation between "proselytization" and "witness." "As an evangelical I draw a sharp distinction between proselytizing and witnessing, rejecting proselytizing as a perversion of witness."[38] Proselytism suggests propaganda, pressure, and coercion; witnessing suggests that the way the individual lives, and describes his faith, is his best method of winning others to it.

Christians who wish to undertake any proselytizing of Jews, even some limited and respectful form of "witnessing," have a heavy historical burden to overcome. Their goodwill may fairly be judged by their willingness to shoulder that burden, that is, to speak to the issue of Christian anti-Semitism and to work seriously to root out remaining anti-Semitic prejudice. Kenneth S. Kantzer, a former editor of the evangelical magazine *Christianity Today* and former dean of Trinity Evangelical School, has argued that evangelical lay leaders and pastors must go well beyond avoiding anti-Semitism themselves and

> ferret out, expose, and actively oppose incipient and overt anti-Semitism that creeps into a society structured for centuries along anti-Semitic lines."[39]

Kantzer has also raised the issue of Jews for Jesus, and warned evangelicals to be careful:

> We abhor any deception in seeking to present Christ to Jews. A small minority of Jewish Christians disguise their Christianity to attract un-

suspecting Jews to accept Christianity. This is deceitful, contrary to the New Testament teaching. Evangelicals have more reasons to oppose this type of deceptive practice than do Jews, but we have often failed them by our silence.[40]

It is fair to ask those who evangelize to meet these standards. It is also fair for Jews to ask evangelicals, seeking as they do to bolster the role of religion in American society, to speak and write about Jews and Judaism with respect and with a decent knowledge of the subject matter. Otherwise, the gap that separates the two communities will never be bridged, and Jewish fears of evangelicals' goals will be impossible to overcome. Otherwise, those Jews who oppose the evangelicals for political reasons—motivated only by a desire to defend liberalism—will continue to enjoy the allegiance of the vast majority of American Jews, still fearful of what conservative Christians really intend for America.

How do evangelicals meet this test? What do they say, and teach their children, about Jews and Judaism? The answer, despite some bits of good news, is discouraging.

What Do Evangelicals Say and Teach About Jews?

In some corners of the evangelical or conservative Christian movement there has been a truly noteworthy effort to understand and answer the concerns of American Jews. In his speech to the Anti-Defamation League in April 1995, Ralph Reed Jr., the executive director of the Christian Coalition, hit these issues head-on. Reed referred to the "undeniable and palpable suspicion—even fear—that divides the Christian community from many American Jews." He acknowledged "that religious conservatives have at times been insensitive and have lacked a full understanding of the horrors experienced by the Jewish people," and that "our political participation is viewed through the lens of this traumatic past." Reed continued:

Those of us who profess the Christian faith must never forget that these horrors occurred not only because of the hatred of a few, but because of the indifference of many . . . in the Christian community. . . . not all who share our faith have demonstrated a sympathy for the burden of this history. This is true not only of the blatant wrong of a few—those who claimed that "God does not hear the prayers of Jews," those who said this is a "Christian nation.". . . It is also true of the thoughtless lapses of many—the use of religious-military metaphors, a false and patronizing philo-semitism, and the belief that being pro-Israel answers for all other insensitivity to Jewish concerns.

He concluded with another reference to Christian anti-Semitism and to the Nazi period, and said,

I reaffirm to you my obligation to teach that history—however painful it may be—to our members and supporters. We will never forget what you have endured as a people and we will do all in our power to ensure that Jews are never again the target of hatred and discrimination.[41]

Reed's comments reflect a remarkable effort to come to grips with Christianity's long history of anti-Semitic thought and action (though, as noted above, this did not spare him a special attack in the very next annual report of the American Jewish Committee). Other evangelicals have gone on record as well, with respect to anti-Semitism. Indeed it is typical now for statements regarding Jews and Judaism to begin with a flat condemnation of anti-Semitism. The Southern Baptist Convention as long ago as 1972 adopted this resolution:

Whereas, this unchristian attitude on the part of many people led to brutal persecution of the Jews in numerous countries and societies, and

Whereas the most flagrant and cruel expression of this spiritual malignancy, the Nazi holocaust, transpired in our generation, and

Whereas, latent anti-Semitism lies barely under the surface in many Western, Christian cultures today, and

Whereas many Christian communions and denominations, including our own, have failed to take a sufficiently vigorous stand against anti-Semitism . . .

Resolved that this Convention go on record as opposed to any and all forms of anti-Semitism; that it declare anti-Semitism unchristian; that we messengers to this Convention pledge ourselves to combat anti-Semitism in every honorable, Christian way [and] work positively to replace all anti-Semitic bias with the Christian attitude and practice of love for Jews who, along with other men, are equally beloved of God.[42]

Still, while their statements denouncing anti-Semitism could fill volumes, the evangelicals too often fall short in their actual teachings about Judaism. Stuart Polly, in his recent, comprehensive study of Protestant teaching materials, concluded that evangelical texts (like most Protestant texts) mention Jews and Judaism constantly when discussing the biblical period, but then the people and the religion disappear. There is little or, more typically, nothing on Christian anti-Semitism and the Holocaust; nothing on new biblical studies about Jesus and his relationship to the Pharisees (which contradict much earlier teaching that presents the Pharisees as unadulteratedly evil); nothing on the development of Judaism as a religion since the birth of Christianity. As Polly put it, "Conservative evangelical curricula view Judaism as a religion that ended with the advent of Jesus or the destruction of the Second Temple in 70 A.D."[43]

Earlier studies of evangelical textbooks showed an even worse pattern. The first, an analysis by Bernhard Olson in 1963, found "prejudice—anti-semitism, in particular" in these texts "across the board."[44] David Rausch, studying the then-current texts two decades later, noted some improvement. "An important finding was that the 'Christ-killer' theme—the most potent religious force in forming anti-Jewish attitudes—was absent from most of these materials. . . . Especially in materials for young children, there was not even a hint of Jewish responsibility for the death of Jesus. Instead, a high regard for the heroes and heroines of the Hebrew Bible was instilled."[45] On the other hand, "although the evangelical publishers of Sunday school literature had provided teaching guides of nearly every conceivable kind to help prepare teachers, not one statement warned the teacher against fostering negative images of Jews and Judaism."[46]

The evangelical community is diverse and churches may choose from a wide variety of available texts. Still, only a few publishers provide the materials used in the vast majority of churches, and conclusions may therefore fairly be drawn. In 1988, David Rausch studied the treatment of the death of Jesus in these materials and found that all too many still teach that the blame lies with the Jews. Material from Gospel Light, a major publisher for fifth and sixth grades, taught that Pontius Pilate was "a mere pawn for the Jewish community's animosity toward Jesus."[47] An adult Sunday school manual for Palm Sunday published by another major evangelical publishing house, David C. Cook, stated that "The Jews continued to bring trumped-up charges against Jesus." The manual continues, "Wrong choices. These two words characterize the chief priests and elders of Israel. At every opportunity they decided against Jesus and for themselves. Their problem was one of attitude. The leaders were comfortable with a religion based on self-righteousness."[48]

What impression can the description of biblical Judaism as "a religion based on self-righteousness" leave? As Rausch concluded, "evangelical Sunday school curricula show definite lack of sensitivity to the anti-Jewish, even anti-Semitic implications of their approach."[49] Similarly, a Gospel Light publication for adults, *Themes*

From Acts by Paul Pierson, has this to say about the role of "the Jews" in Jesus' death:

> Yet the Jews, led by their priests, had engineered His condemnation and handed Jesus over to pagan rulers to be crucified. . . . They and their leaders had not only rejected the long-awaited Messiah; they had put themselves clearly into opposition to God by crucifying Him! . . . [The sin and its effects were] both collective and individual, national and personal.[50]

Of this language Rausch correctly asked, "While one could make a strong case Dr. Pierson is not anti-Semitic, his book (as so many others) lacks sensitivity to the historic problems such statements have caused the Jewish people, and he shirks his responsibility as an educator to correct such impressions."[51]

The recent Polly study found that too little had changed in evangelical texts. There are the always welcome condemnations of anti-Semitism; and entirely absent is the suggestion that the Jewish diaspora is a punishment by God for the rejection of Jesus. But, "the charge of deicide is very much present . . . in the conservative Christian denominations."[52] Two examples suffice: A Lutheran Church-Missouri Synod teacher's manual states that "They [the Jewish leaders] refused to accept Christ as God-revealed and indicted him as a traitor because He proclaimed a loving God who required and provided a righteousness that was far superior to the burdensome religion they embraced and imposed upon the people."[53] And a Southern Baptist Convention text is even worse. "Paul described what the Jews did. *They* condemned Christ; *they* executed him." (Italics are in the original.) The Jews "failed to recognize Him. Instead they crucified Him. Jesus was executed illegally. Pontius Pilate gave his permission, but Jewish pressure brought it about. . . . How did the Jewish leaders fail to recognize Jesus? Probably the same way people fail to recognize Him today."[54]

Thus while anti-Semitism is denounced, contempt for Judaism has not been excised. Polly describes the Assemblies of God's materials as providing "a comprehensive anti-Jewish perspective."[55] A Southern Baptist text teaches students that "The zeal of the Jews that was without knowledge [of Christ] turned into legalistic fanaticism as they took religious pride in opposing Christ."[56]

There are some materials that treat Jews and Judaism well. In the Lutheran Church (both the Evangelical Lutheran Church of America and the more evangelical Missouri Synod), material prepared for special courses about Jews and Judaism is often excellent and is sometimes compiled with the help of a rabbi. But the knowledge and understanding shown in these special courses, often for self-selected adults, does not filter through into materials made generally available for children in Sunday school literature.[57]

Similarly, it is fair to ask how widely that superb speech by Ralph Reed will be distributed, and how many pastors will use it as the basis for a sermon or a Sunday School class. Reed, after all, is a political rather than a religious leader, and a layman rather than a leader of the evangelical clergy. Will his speech be a model for future comments by leaders of the evangelical churches themselves?

Polly's study concludes overall that there has been progress in evangelical texts but far too little of it. Too often Judaism is presented as a dead religion, superseded by Christianity, and Jews are held responsible for Jesus' death; too seldom is anything said about Judaism as a living religion, the modern state of Israel, or the history of Christian anti-Semitism, including the Holocaust.

Does it matter? When evangelicals are taught little about today's Jews or modern Judaism, and come into little contact with either, it is reasonable to fear that the negative Gospel-based images of Jews and Judaism they are given will prove more powerful than the warnings against anti-Semitism they also receive. Theological anti-Judaism can become Christian anti-Semitism, as it has so often throughout history.[58] Evangelicals are sending a clear message against anti-Semitism, but thus far their efforts to reform their presentation of Judaism have been extremely weak. The way to deal with the teaching of contempt is to stop it, not to accompany it with preachings of brotherhood. In this, the evangelicals lag far behind the Roman Catholic Church, and behind the mainline Protestant churches as well.

It is in this context that some of the more controversial comments by the Rev. Pat Robertson should be seen. In recent years, Robertson has been the subject of countless critiques that are more political than religious in nature, the Anti-Defamation League's report among them. But like too many of his colleagues in the evangelical movement, he has paid little attention to what his remarks about Jews and Judaism may mean to his followers. If there is no anti-Semitism in his words, there is a carelessness, even a blindness, that Robertson must address if he desires Jews to view him as a well-intentioned, nonthreatening religious and political leader.

Some of this is a matter of style rather than content, but just as likely to offend: Robertson's comparisons of the plight of religious Christians in America to that of Jews in Nazi Germany will shock not only Jews but many other Americans as well: "To many people, Christians seem somehow out of pace with the spirit of the age. Our protests and warnings are an annoyance. . . . we can expect the same treatment that the Jews experienced in Nazi Germany."[59]

Other statements, however benign in their intent, can inflame anti-Semitism. Robertson sometimes uses the term "Christian" in a way that cannot help but worry Jews, as when he writes that "Christians should be wary of placing their hopes in non-Christian men and in programs of secular political parties."[60] The context suggests that "Christian" here does not mean "Christian as opposed to Jew" but rather "truly believing, God-fearing people as opposed to irreligious or atheistic people." Still, seeing the word "Christian," a reader could interpret such a statement as a warning against voting for Jews for public office.

Similarly, Robertson's public musings in 1989 about what he viewed as excessive Jewish militancy (in the struggle against the building of a Carmelite convent at Auschwitz) raised a question many Jews often ask themselves: do such public arguments with large Christian groups threaten to give rise to anti-Semitism? Robertson wrote that "a strident minority within a minority of 5,000,000" was attempting the "systematic vilification, weakening, and ultimate suppression of the majority point of view from society," added that this would "enrage and alienate" Christians, and warned of "a Christian backlash."[61] Even if it can be said that he was genuinely puzzled by the strength of Jewish opposition to the convent, and truly worried about a backlash, his language must strike Jews as more likely to create than to defuse one. Robertson was guilty here of gross insensitivity to the impact of his language.

Finally, he has occasionally borrowed language from traditional Christian anti-Semitic stereotypes. In his 1991 book, *The New World Order,* he wrote of the influence of "European bankers" and a "tightly knit cabal" who conspire to run our affairs, both familiar anti-Semitic lines. His references to the purported role of the Rothschild family follow the same path. In writing this book he relied on sources that are plainly anti-Semitic and should never be the basis of a serious political or religious work.

Thus Pat Robertson can be seen to fit the profile of the evangelical with respect to Jews and Judaism. He offers very welcome statements of support for Israel and strong opposition to anti-Semitism, but he also sometimes evinces a remarkable insensitivity in maintaining old and damaging stereotypes about Jews and their religion. An editorial about evangelical-Jewish relations published fifteen years ago in *Christianity Today* set a high standard for evangelicals: "It is not enough just to condemn anti-Semitism in the past and remain aloof from anti-Semitic causes. Evangelical leaders and pastors must also use their teaching ministries to present solid instruction as to the antibiblical and anti-Christian nature of all anti-Semitic attitudes or actions."[62] Fifteen years later—and despite some real progress—the evidence suggests that standard is still not being met.

On the other hand, much of whatever conversation there is between Jews and evangelical Christians is about precisely the *wrong* subjects. All too many Jewish groups act not as Jewish entities but rather as liberal political bodies, taking on the evangelicals on such matters as gun control or gay rights. Worse yet, conservative Christians have been defamed with broad-brush denunciations, guilt by association, and conclusions rooted more in politics than religion.

Such behavior comes at a great cost, for it is that much more difficult for evangelicals and Jews to cooperate where the subject matter is religious in nature, where there are some serious problems, and where real progress may be possible. Both as to missionary work and Sunday school teachings about Judaism, some conservative Christian groups have shown new sensitivity—the speech by Ralph Reed being the best example of it—and it should be encouraged and expanded. *Here* is important work for the national Jewish organizations, directly affecting the interests of all American Jews. But a person cannot smear someone Monday and expect his cooperation Tuesday, as leaders of the ADL learned when the National Association of Evangelicals pulled back from a joint project with them aimed at revising textbook treatment of Jews.

Jews and evangelicals have skewed visions of each other, which are frequently based on ignorance. What evangelicals learn about Jews and Judaism is too often inadequate, biased, and capable of fostering anti-Semitism. Yet it is clear from the survey data that evangelicals do not at all match the typical Jewish portrait of them as a group of anti-Semites and Christian triumphalists who present a danger to Jewish interests. It is painful to contemplate the opportunities for better knowledge of each other, the definition of common interests, and productive cooperation that may be lost if these two groups cannot work more closely together.

From the Jewish perspective, the chance to work closely with Christian groups whose size and influence are growing, and which are strongly pro-Israel, should be enormously attractive. With the Jewish community shrinking, the recruitment of American Christians to support Israel is one obvious goal. On public policy matters of direct Jewish interest—church-state issues and prayer in schools—their voice is enormously important and the opportunity to clarify for them the worries and concerns of Jews is extremely valuable.

There will be more, rather than less, religion in American public life in the coming years—whether the Jewish community likes it or not. From remarks by President Clinton, to the most recent Supreme Court decisions on religion, to the very growth of the evangelical movement itself, all evidence points in that direction, and there is even powerful support for a constitutional amendment permitting prayer in schools. In the summer of 1995 the Clinton administration, perhaps in an effort to head off such an amendment, released guidelines for public school officials that stressed just how much religion was, even now, permissible in the schools. Students "have the right to engage in individual or group prayer . . . during the school day" and "may also speak to, and attempt to persuade, their peers about religious topics." The statement advised school officials, however, to "intercede to stop student speech that constitutes harassment aimed at a student or group of students" and to "ensure that no student is in any way coerced to participate in religious activity." The statement also noted that "public schools may not provide religious instruction, but they may teach about religion, including the Bible."[63]

These principles will seem to many American Jews to provide a menu for trouble, for in their interpretation and implementation there are so many ways in which the feelings, as well as the rights, of Jewish students may be affected. But there are advantages to be had here for the Jewish community as well. For in working with both evangelical and nonevangelical Christian groups to explain their fears, Jews can seek and find ways to avoid having them turn into bruising confrontations.

This is so clearly in the interest of the American Jewish community that, at the very least, its members must not let political biases interfere. It is far more important for American Jews to work with evangelicals on their understanding of Judaism than to denounce them for their views on environmentalism, capital punishment, or funding for National Public Radio.

Jews and Christians in America

Within the American Jewish community there remains considerable suspicion, not to say hostility, toward Christianity, though there is little said about this phenomenon. From a certain point of view, it may seem a serviceable prejudice in that it may contribute to a stronger sense of Jewish separateness and thus to the strengthening of Jewish identity. But that is a sad foundation for Jewish cohesiveness, and it should be anathema to Jews who pride themselves on fighting bigotry in all its forms.

The last quarter century has seen profound changes in Christian attitudes toward Jews and Judaism. These changes have not been matched in Jewish attitudes toward Christianity. While many Christian denominations now acknowledge that the covenant of Abraham still endures, American Jews too seldom either know about or appreciate Christianity and its teachings.

At the very least, Jews should understand the role of Christianity in spreading knowledge of the Torah. The Jewish theologian Franz Rosenzweig wrote that "Our recognition of Christianity rests, in fact, upon its recognition of us. It is the Torah, ultimately, which is spread abroad by Bible societies to the most distant lands."[64] But this is only a reflection of the insight of Maimonides, who wrote eight hundred years ago in the Mishneh Torah that through the spread of Christianity, "the messianic hope, the Torah, and the commandments have become familiar topics—topics of conversation among the inhabitants of far isles and many peoples."[65] Unfortunately, Jewish-Christian dialogue remains a narrow conversation among experts whose advances are too often simply unknown to most American Jews—and Christians.

It was difficult for most Jews to take any positive view of Christianity while Christians were threatening them. Today, in a moment of historic reversal, Christians are becoming more respectful of Judaism than are Jews of Christianity. This should be a sobering thought for the American Jewish community. Jewish interests and morality alike compel the Jewish community to prevent politics and prejudice from determining its attitude toward Christianity in America.

Yet Jews may still legitimately ask whether the picture of Christian attitudes toward Jews and Judaism presented here does not justify a certain nervousness on the part of Jews. Given the lacunae in Christian understanding of modern Judaism and of the place of the state of Israel in the hearts of many Jews, given the survival of objectionable references to Jews in Christian texts, and given the proselytization campaigns of some evangelical groups, is there not plenty for Jews to fear if religion comes to hold a larger place in American life? Even those Jews who grant the positive role religion can play in reinforcing civic virtue and private morality may also wonder whether the costs to them will not far outweigh the benefits.

The answer is no. The real issue is not whether Christian America earns high or low marks on exams about Judaism but whether the Christian behavior that remains objectionable actually threatens Jews and Jewish interests properly defined—and whether driving religion from public life will help eliminate or change that behavior.

If proselytization efforts are deeply offensive, they are probably the less effective for that. Indeed, the vast majority of Americans of Jewish heritage who are now Christian crossed that line not at the urging of a group like Jews for Jesus but because one generation drifted away from Judaism, and, with intermarriage, the next left it behind entirely. They abandoned Judaism not out of religious zeal but because of its absence—whether in colonial Charleston or modern-day Denver. Jews should object to proselytization efforts targeted at them *in principle:* not because in the United States such efforts have ever been effective, but because they display—as they have through the ages—contempt for Judaism.

The same is true of Christian religious and educational materials that present Judaism in a critical light. The impact of such literature on Christian anti-Semitism is difficult to discern. Anti-Semitism has been declining in America during the years when many denominations have rewritten their texts to take a more positive view of Judaism, and perhaps the new material has produced this effect. But poll data do not suggest that evangelical Christians, whose textual treatments of Judaism are typically worse, are more anti-Semitic than Roman Catholics or Protestants from mainline denominations. With regard to these texts, cause and effect cannot be demonstrated.

So it is with religion's role in American life and the Jew's place in this society, more generally. Jews believe they will be at risk if religion becomes a more visible factor in American life, but they cannot demonstrate why anyone should believe this. When all is said and done, Jews do not believe that a more religious America threatens them because studies of Christian Sunday school texts or missionary societies concluded that this was so. They do not believe it threatens them because Christian anti-Semitism in America is growing, for it is not. They cannot argue that Jews will be unable to thrive in America if the secularist court decisions and social trends of recent decades are reversed, for the Jewish community did indeed thrive in the "bad old days" and in fact did not then face the demographic problems that now plague it.

No, American Jews believe simply as an article of faith that a more religious society threatens them—and this has been a much more powerful credo for the American Jew than any of the laws of Moses. Their adherence to secularism does not result from any survey research, sociological analysis, or political science, much less from their religion. It does not emerge from any insights into modern Christianity or for that matter modern American life. It is founded in fear, and though that fear can easily be explained by Jewish history, it cannot be defended by reference to Jewish interests today. It freezes American Jews into a pattern of thought and behavior that is unfair to their neighbors and damaging to their own future.

It is, to say the least, morally offensive to see Jewish groups displaying a combination of class prejudice, political intolerance, and real difficulty coming to grips with Christianity. Religious fervor is being associated with ignorance and lack of education. Christians whose faithfulness to their religion, and ability to keep their children faithful to it, should be a model for Jews, are instead seen as bumpkins and bigots.

Chapter 5

INTERMARRIAGE

HOWEVER fearful of a Christian society contemporary Jews may claim to be, they have in dangerously increasing numbers been voting otherwise with their feet. One of the ironies of the demographic crisis with which this book began is that the very Jewish groups who most loudly profess their anxiety about Christians are, with a frequency never before seen in all of Jewish history, marrying them.

Assimilation by intermarriage is, of course, a major contributor to the Americanization of many ethnic groups. But for a long time, for the reasons discussed in Chapter Two, this did not apply in any significant measure to the Jews. Now, however, the data have become startling. The National Jewish Population Study of 1990, for instance, has found quite simply that a majority of Jewish marriages are now intermarriages. The debate over intermarriage set off by this announcement has proven to be not only critically important in itself but offers perhaps the single most important insight into the condition of American Judaism today.

The survey found that of Jews who married after 1985, 52 percent married non-Jews; but while the intermarriage rate accelerated, the conversion rate was *declining*.[1] The proportion of non-Jewish spouses converting, which had been over 20 percent in the 1940s, was down to 5 percent by the time of the study.[2]

The result: the majority of new "Jewish" households formed in the United States now consist of one Jew and one gentile who has not converted to Judaism. And as the years go by and that intermarriage rate is repeated or raised each year, it's obvious that a greater and greater percentage of American Jews will be living in mixed households. In 1957, 94 percent of American Jews lived in exclusively Jewish households. Today only two-thirds do.[3]

Viewed against the very low American Jewish intermarriage rates of the past, this has been an unpleasant surprise—indeed a shock—for the community. But it ought not to be a surprise in this open society: the melting pot continues to do its job. Given the failure of "Jewishness" and absent a strong new commitment to Judaism, rising intermarriage is inevitable for Jews, as it is for other groups within the U.S. population.

Among Japanese Americans the intermarriage rate is about 50 percent now, meaning that half of the marriages entered into by Japanese Americans are with other Japanese Americans, and half are not.[4] Among Chinese Americans as well, the rate continues to rise. Foreign-born Chinese Americans most often marry others from their group, and a Chinese American community living with high immigration, such as the one in New York City, has an intermarriage rate of only 25 percent. But in Los Angeles it is now over 40 percent, and in the older Chinese community in Hawaii it is now nearly 75 percent.[5]

The rate of intermarriage among European ethnic groups in the United States is just as high or higher. In 1963–64, about 59 percent of Italian Americans chose people of similar, unmixed Italian descent to marry; the intermarriage rate was, then, already 41 percent. Fifteen years later, by 1979, the majority of Italian Americans were marrying people from outside the community. To measure it another way, in 1979 only 6 percent of Italian Americans *over age 65* were of mixed heritage, and 94 percent were "pure Italian." But for those children *under five years of age,* only 19.5 percent were "pure Italian," and 80.5 percent were of mixed heritage.

And more and more Italian Americans married out of their faith. While 73 percent of the first generation in the United States married Catholics, 45 percent of the third generation did so. The majority married Protestants.[6]

Data from the 1990 census indicate that for Italian Americans then in their thirties (born between 1956 and 1965), the intermarriage rate is 73 percent. It is as high for Irish and Polish Americans. The Irish American intermarriage rate for people in their thirties was 65 percent; the Polish American rate was a striking 84 percent.[7] Richard D. Alba, a student of ethnic patterns, summed it up in his 1985 book, *Italian Americans:* "among almost all groups, one can see a spreading pattern of intermarriage, testimony to the trivial nature of remaining group differences and guarantee of additional assimilation."[8]

The fact that intermarriage is so widespread casts a new light on Jewish intermarriage. For one thing, it rules out older ways of accounting for the decision to intermarry: rebellion against one's parents, for example, or the search for higher social status. Jews have high enough social status nowadays and do not need to marry out to raise it. Nor, with such high rates of intermarriage, is it reasonable to view falling in love with a non-Jew as a psychodrama designed to hurt one's parents. In a society this integrated, where Jews come into contact with non-Jews so often and so intimately, it isn't surprising that the intermarriage rate is high. It is predictable.

It is also logical to expect that it will continue to rise—all other things being equal. Among ethnic groups, intermarriage rates rise with each generation. It's natural: as the family's arrival in America becomes more distant in time, older customs are lost, fellow

Americans seem less strange and different, and patterns of work and residence coalesce with those of others. Americans become more American, more like one another, less separated by variant family histories, differing faiths, and, even (in the Japanese and Chinese cases) by different races. In *Mixed Blood,* his 1989 book on the subject, Paul Spickard concluded that "the pattern of Jewish outmarriage over three generations in America was like that of Japanese-Americans: little outmarriage in the immigrant group, more in the second generation, and substantially more in the third."[9] So the rising intermarriage rate among Jewish families reflects, first of all, the simple fact that many have by now been in America for a century.

But rising intermarriage rates reflect two other things as well: Christian attitudes toward marrying Jews, and American—including American Jewish—attitudes toward social integration and individual autonomy.

Jews tend to see intermarriage as the decision of a Jew to marry a Christian, but the reverse is true as well. Surely intermarriage rates were held down, in the past, by anti-Semitism and the refusal of Christians to consider Jews as eligible marriage partners. As part of the general decline in anti-Semitism in America, that Christian resistance to marrying Jews has diminished greatly. In 1950, for example, a 57 percent majority of Christians disapproved of marriages between Christians and Jews. By 1983 only 12 percent of Protestants and 6 percent of Catholics were still against it, and teenagers approved Jewish-Christian and Protestant-Catholic marriages by the same proportions.[10] This age-old protection against intermarriage is evaporating.

This is to be expected in a society with American ideals: intermarriage reflects the goal of the open society, the melting pot that dissolves our differences into a new common nationality. Writing in

1782, the French visitor Crèvecoeur noted this in his *Letters from an American Farmer:*

> What then is the American, this strange new man? He is either a European or the descendant of a European, hence that strange mixture of blood, which you will find in no other country. I could point out to you a family whose grandfather was an Englishman, whose wife was Dutch, whose son married a French woman, and whose present four sons have four wives of different nations. He is an American, who, leaving behind him all his ancient prejudices and manners, receives new ones from the new mode of life he has embraced.[11]

More than two centuries later, his description still rings true. With this social ideal before it, American society can fairly be said to foster intermarriage.

And intermarriage reflects yet another ideal, one much more contemporary than the mixing of immigrant groups: individual autonomy. The decision to put certain marriage partners off limits requires subordinating personal attraction and autonomy to other loyalties, usually to a racial or religious group and to a family's preferences. This is not the spirit of the age. The idea that one should sacrifice one's personal happiness to such old-fashioned considerations is a hard sell in America today.

Third parties who might once have interfered to stop a marriage out of the community are now much less likely to do so. Churches and parents, once the customary intervenors, are far less willing to play that role today. Parents as well as children now see parental interference in the choice of a child's mate as illegitimate, and in any event unmarried children no longer all live at home in constant contact with their parents. Churches used to intervene; once upon a time, the Catholic Church, the Mormon Church, and even some mainline Protestant bodies like the Lutherans made serious efforts to stop intermarriage and even refused to celebrate marriages out of the faith, but that too is a thing of the past. Perhaps the churches are afraid of losing the new couple as members; perhaps they are simply reflecting the spirit of the age as well. The outcome, in any event, is that when in America a young mixed couple moves toward engagement and marriage, it is unlikely that anyone will rise up to try to stop them.

Religious differences are no longer a socially acceptable barrier to marriage, any more than ethnic, national, or racial differences are. Americans, and especially American liberals, have understood that America is a country where individuals must be judged as marriage partners on their individual merits, not by their group membership. In fact intermarriage "signifies the fulfillment of the Jew's demand for acceptance as an individual—a demand he has been making since the Emancipation."[12]

But this creates an exquisite difficulty for Jews, who at the same time understand that intermarriage will lead to demographic disaster. Jonathan Sarna, a professor of American Jewish history at Brandeis University, put it very plainly:

> Where once . . . Jews and other Americans held congruent views on intermarriage, views strongly supportive of endogamy, *Jews today are all alone in their views, separated from the pro-intermarriage mainstream by a huge cultural chasm.*[13]

To oppose intermarriage, he went on, would be to set themselves against the mainstream of American life. It would be to place separatism and particularism, group identity and group survival, above social integration, individualism, and liberal ideals. How can the Jewish community fight intermarriage without seeming to reject marriages with fellow citizens on grounds that may seem illiberal, even sectarian? How can Jews urge their children to judge fellow Americans not, as Martin Luther King once put it, on the content of their character but on the color of their skin—or the accident of birth in or out of a particular religious community? How can Jews define Judaism, in this day and age, not as a belief system each individual may embrace or reject but as a covenant imposing obligations on a single community—indeed a community of birth, not of choice?

Most Jews, apart from the Orthodox, would be very uncomfortable taking such a stance. So they don't. After all the talk within the American Jewish community about an intermarriage crisis, one might have expected Jews to be fighting intermarriage. Sarna may be right in saying that Jews' views of intermarriage are negative, but what do they do about it? Accept it, rationalize it, and make believe that its dire demographic consequences are not inevitable.

The Intermarriage Lobby

Members of the Jewish community, in greater and greater numbers, have begun to accept intermarriage, some with such enthusiasm that they may be described as favoring it. Some argue that it will have little negative demographic impact or even a positive impact. Others may be motivated by pessimism, suggesting that if intermarriage cannot be stopped we must accommodate to it. Still others are driven by family matters—a child who has intermarried. All present as their central and very powerful idea that the Jewish community must reach out to mixed couples or give up the chance to achieve conversions and to have the children raised as Jews. Scolding, rejection, and exclusion, they argue, will be counterproductive.

In fact, most Jews have accepted intermarriage as inevitable. A 1989 poll by the American Jewish Committee revealed that only 36 percent of Jews would now oppose or strongly oppose a child's marriage with a non-Jew. Four percent would encourage it and 53 percent would accept the decision and remain neutral. Steven

Cohen, a professor at the Hebrew University of Jerusalem and the sociologist who conducted the study, summed up its findings: "most American Jews have made their peace with mixed marriage."[14]

So roughly one-third of Jews would oppose a child's intermarriage, and two-thirds would not. When asked what their ideals for their children were, 81 percent wanted their children to feel good about being Jewish, 73 percent wanted their grandsons circumcised, but only 51 percent checked off "marrying a Jew." Cohen could not help remarking that according to these results, Jewish grandparents are more interested in their grandsons' circumcisions than in their actual religion.

Whatever their ideological position on intermarriage, few Jews today will do what their grandparents would routinely have done if a child married a gentile, namely sit shiva, or regard that child as dead and engage in mourning rituals for him or her. Love will overpower whatever disapproval or disappointment may be felt, and family members will most likely opt for inclusiveness. There will be talk of a possible later conversion, or perhaps of the hope that the grandchildren can still be raised as Jews. The fact is that reactions to intermarriage are very often determined not by intellectual analyses but by personal pressures.

No one wants to "write off" a child or grandchild. The problem comes in separating the demands of parental love from those of the community. While Charlotte Holstein was head of the Jewish Communal Affairs Commission of the American Jewish Committee, her daughter was married to a Catholic. When she chaired the commission's discussions about the AJC's position on intermarriage, she found this theme resonating throughout. "It was my impression," she wrote in describing the discussions, "that the difficulty rested in the fact that individuals still could not separate what they felt was a personal matter from what was in the best interests of the Jewish community. The two factors were indistinguishable in the minds of many."[15] As a result, acknowledged Egon Mayer, one of the Reform movement's foremost students of intermarriage and director of the Center for Jewish Studies at the Graduate School of the City University of New York, many Jews "want their leaders to mirror in communal policies the emotional acceptance that most express for their children's marriage choice."[16]

Of all Jews, Reform Jews are the most likely to have to face the impact of mixed marriage in their personal lives. This is not surprising, as members of the Reform Jewish community are more likely to intermarry than Conservative or Orthodox Jews. Jewish separatism hardly appeals to the liberal principles, the universalist values, the humanism that Reform Judaism champions, and it is disarmed ideologically for the battle against mixed marriage. Instead, Reform has adopted a kind of neutralism in the struggle against intermarriage, reflected in the words of Egon Mayer: the Jewish community should be "as open and welcoming to our own interfaith families as America has been open and welcoming to us. . . . And this requires us to be as respectful of the philosophical and life style choices of interfaith families as we would want them to be of more traditional Jewish choices."[17] By this logic, the Jewish community must value equally the "life style choice" of having a Christmas tree and that of having a seder, and above all the "life style choice" of marrying within the faith and that of marrying outside it.

The intermarriage rate among Reform Jews has been estimated at 60 percent.[18] According to a 1990 Brandeis University study, "In many communities mixed married households comprise a substantial presence within the Reform population: of households which define themselves as Reform Jews, one-fifth of Dallas and one-quarter of San Francisco and Boston households are mixed married."[19] Professor Jack Wertheimer of the Jewish Theological Seminary, combining the high rate of intermarriage and Reform efforts to re-cruit these families for temple membership, asked what the future looked like. "Reform leaders openly acknowledge," he reported, "that as a result of these two trends, within the next few decades over half the families in Reform temples will be intermarried cou-ples and their children."[20]

Nor is this phenomenon limited to inactive Reform Jews; it touches members of the Reform leadership elites just as thoroughly. A study of the leaders attending a recent Reform biennial national convention found that almost one-third of their children had inter-married, a tenfold increase in one generation. Needless to say, these Reform leaders are the most accepting of intermarriage and the most in favor of having rabbis officiate at mixed marriages.[21] More-over, the Brandeis study concluded, "a growing proportion of the delegates to future Biennials will be participants in conversionary marriages and intermarriages."[22] About 25 percent of Reform *lead-ers* under age forty were already involved in mixed marriages.

In sum, despite its occasional rhetoric and hand-wringing, the American Jewish community—and most of all its largest single component, Reform Judaism—is experiencing more and more in-termarriages, and fighting them less and less. A good example of this new attitude was provided in 1995 by the United Jewish Ap-peal, the key organization for fund-raising on behalf of Israel and one that reaches all elements of American Jewry, when it sponsored its first "mission" to Israel for intermarried couples.[23] Such missions are carefully orchestrated trips whose goal, from the UJA perspec-tive, is to arouse or cement the travelers' commitment to Israel and to charitable contributions through UJA. On this trip, Saturday was divided between a Jewish sabbath service and a visit to the Church of the Nativity in Bethlehem. UJA spokesmen called the mission an effective form of outreach; critics argued that the entire effort seemed to give a UJA sanction to intermarriage, and showed that intermarriage has now become an accepted part of life in the major Jewish institutions.

Instead of wrenching changes in behavior that might actually reduce the rate of intermarriage, the community seems satisfied by a new vision: maintaining Jewish identity in a mixed marriage and keeping the children Jewish. If the children and grandchildren of intermarried Jews remain Jews or become Jews, after all, the demographic battle will be won and there will be no demographic problem. But do those children stay Jewish?

Jewish Identity and the Children of Intermarriage

What are the effects of intermarriage on the children raised in one, and—to the extent that data are available—on the grandchildren of those original intermarriers? Everyone in the Jewish community seems to know of a mixed marriage that produced a conversion, a newly Jewish spouse who is devout and observant, or children who are more religious than their Jewish grandparents. Such anecdotal evidence proves the point that generalizations never cover all cases. Statistics cannot predict and do not control what will happen to one individual, one marriage, one set of children. But they do tell what is happening to the Jewish community as a whole.*

One must ask, to begin with, how many children are now being raised in intermarried homes. Given that the rising intermarriage rate has passed 50 percent, perhaps it is not surprising that—for what must be the first time in American Jewish history—there are

---

*It is important to note that intermarriage is a term with two subsets: mixed marriage and conversionary marriage. A mixed marriage is one between a Jew and a non-Jew, who both remain in their original religions during the marriage. A conversionary marriage is one in which the non-Jewish partner converts to Judaism, and as such it is not a mixed marriage. These two kinds of intermarriage must be distinguished to judge the impact on children.

more young children now being raised in intermarried than in all-Jewish households. Of children in the age group zero-to-nine who are living with two parents, there are 410,000 living in households where both parents are Jewish, and 479,000 living in households where one parent is Jewish and the other is not.[24]

And how are children in intermarried families raised? Twenty-eight percent of the children of mixed marriages are being raised as Jews, while 41 percent are raised as non-Jews and 31 percent with no religion at all.[25] As these numbers suggest, most mixed couples do not give their children much of a Jewish education. Among wholly Jewish households, 70 percent of the children get some Jewish education. In mixed families, the number drops to 20 percent, and 80 percent receive no Jewish education whatsoever.[26] As a Brandeis study concluded, these findings

> have grave implications for the future Jewish identification of the population. Erosion of numbers because of lack of Jewish education and its corollary of Jewish identity is certain to continue since so few children being brought up in mixed households receive any kind of formal Jewish schooling.[27]

Most Jews know instinctively that a mixed household will have a hard time conveying a strong Jewish identity. A 1992 report done for the American Jewish Committee corroborates their instincts, reaching stark and sad conclusions:

> Despite the hopes and assumptions, Jewish identification does not fare well in mixed marriages. . . . In all, the data indicate that mixed marriage and the level of Jewish identification are strongly negatively related. So few mixed-marrieds manifest a high level of Jewish identification, and denominational connection makes so little impact in this regard, that mixed marriage must be regarded as a virtual bar to the achievement of a high level of Jewish identification.[28]

In fact, only 20 percent of mixed households celebrate Jewish holidays, while 54 percent celebrate Christian holidays.[29] Nearly two-thirds of mixed families have a Christmas tree, and no Jewish holiday—not even Hanukkah—is celebrated by so high a percentage.[30] There is "a substantial amount of Christian practice" within the homes even of leaders of Reform Judaism married to non-Jews.[31] The children in a mixed household will have a set of Christian grandparents, aunts, uncles, and cousins. They will have a prolonged and intimate exposure to non-Jewish culture and a mixed cultural and ethnic identity. Their parents may be indifferent to whether the children think of themselves as Jews, and indeed only 26 percent of parents in mixed marriages say it is important to them that their children identify as Jews.[32] These parents are very unlikely to oppose mixed marriage for their children, having themselves entered into one.

From all of this it is safe to predict that the intermarriage rate of *children* of mixed marriages is high. The scarce data that exist indicate that it is 90 percent. As logic suggests, this is true beyond the Jewish community as well: a study based on the 1980 census concluded that "we know that persons of mixed origin are more likely to outmarry than are compatriots of unmixed origin."[33]

Despite the hopes of many in the Jewish community, then, the effect of mixed marriages on children is evident. Only 28 percent are raised as Jews, and an even smaller percentage marry Jews. This suggests that mixed marriage will produce more mixed marriage, and fewer Jews in the following generation. A three-generational study of the Jews of Philadelphia found that no grandchildren of mixed marriages continued to identify as Jews.[34]

But there is more: children of mixed marriages tend to have a special view of Jewishness and Judaism. They see it as a personal choice, and 80 percent say that religion is "a purely private matter." The great majority do not believe that participating in organized

Jewish life is a necessary way of expressing Jewishness, and 81 percent of the children of mixed marriages say "belonging to a Jewish community" is not important.[35] Children of mixed marriages tend, then, to accept something like a Christian definition of religion, in which personal faith is the key and community membership and solidarity are of much less importance. Religion is to most of them a matter of belief, not of community.

To sum up, the children of mixed marriages, having mixed ethnic and religious heritages, are likely to feel less allegiance to the Jewish community, and are less likely to identify as Jews and to seek to marry Jews. For a community as small as the Jewish community, now under 2 percent of the population and declining, and living less and less in large and dense Jewish communities, there is also the matter of availability of Jewish marriage partners. Data demonstrate clearly that Jewish intermarriage rates are highest in areas where Jews are scarcest. Richard Alba, in his study of Italian Americans, explained that

> intermarriage is to a very important degree a function of the size of the group. The smaller it is, the more difficult it is for an individual to find a suitable spouse within its boundaries and hence the greater is the probability of intermarriage. . . . high rates of intermarriage in the present guarantee high rates in the future because they deplete ethnic communities of a substantial part of the next generation, in effect reducing the size of the group.[36]

Thus intermarriage is a multigenerational phenomenon with an innate tendency to get worse. Assimilation steadily increases from generation to generation in what's been called a chain effect.[37] Even when the Jew who marries a non-Jew remains Jewish, his or her children are much less likely to do so and the grandchildren even less likely.

The Conversion Myth

Jews who are seeking an escape from the growing demographic crisis often turn to another theory, that conversion may solve the problem. Conversion of the non-Jewish spouse, it is argued, produces a wholly Jewish household, and would seem likely to produce more Jews in the next generation. Does it?

Yes and no. Children of conversionary families get more Jewish education, have a greater Jewish identity, and marry Jews more often than children of mixed marriages. In *Children of Intermarriage,* Mayer reported that only 24 percent of the children of mixed marriages identify as Jews, while 84 percent of the children of conversionary marriages do.[38] Often, as both data and anecdotal evidence suggest, the convert is a dutiful and observant Jew. Many Jews can tell a story about a converted spouse who *wants* to attend synagogue or keep kosher, and is held back by the resistance of the spouse who was born a Jew.

But converts nevertheless still bring with them traditions alien to Judaism. For one thing, like all non-Jews who marry Jews, they can provide their children with a loving set of Christian relatives whose lives may offer an alternative faith, diminishing the Jewish identification and affiliation of the children. Converts seem to have difficulty conveying to their children their own sense of unique affiliation to Judaism: 22 percent, for example, still erect a Christmas tree.

Over the generations the numbers are not good. One study found that although children of conversionary marriages did not enter mixed marriages any more often than did born Jews, in *none* of the cases where the children of converts married non-Jews did the non-Jews convert. The *grand*children of converts, then, unlike their own children, would grow up in mixed households. While 86 percent of husbands and wives in conversionary couples joined

synagogues, only 38 percent of their children did.[39] The study of
Reform Jewish leaders mentioned earlier asked converts how they
would feel about their children converting back to Christianity.
Sarna commented on the results and spelled out the implications:

> [m]ore than 50 percent of the converts responding—leaders, I remind
> you—would not even be bothered a great deal if their children *converted
> to Christianity*. There is here a world of difference between converts and
> born Jews. . . . the data we now have at hand should serve as a dire
> warning: *Unless we act decisively, many of today's converts will be one-
> generation Jews—Jews with non-Jewish parents and non-Jewish children*.[40]

Today it is common to hear that all Jews are "Jews By Choice,"
and those who use that phrase are talking about the fact that we all
live in a free and open society. We can choose to disaffiliate, to
change religion, or to live without religion altogether. This is an especially appealing concept to converts, who have acted upon it in
their own lives. So it would be a lot to expect a convert to reject the
act of intermarriage and conversion, which he or she undertook to
create the very family in question. And in fact, only 24 percent of
converts say they would discourage intermarriage by a child, while
69 percent say they would not.[41] If this is not much worse than the
figures for the Jewish community in general (36 percent would discourage, 53 percent would not), it *is* worse; and it indicates that the
great majority of converts take the view that the choice they made
is not binding on their children.

The problem is that this is not the traditional Jewish view, which
posits a *community* of Jews whose religion claims that Jews live in a
covenant with God that imposes special obligations upon them.
Prime among these is the duty imposed in Deuteronomy 6:7 and
repeated every day in one of Judaism's most important prayers, the
Sh'ma: "Thou shalt teach them diligently unto thy children." The
Jewish view has always been that every Jew has an obligation to

instruct his or her children in *Judaism,* not in the virtues of free thinking. Judaism imposes obligations binding on one and on one's offspring, and it is this that many converts seem to refuse or at least to be unsuccessful in transmitting from one generation to the next.

It is easy to conclude that conversionary households are vastly preferable to mixed households when it comes to Jewish identity, and that the community should encourage conversion. It is easier still to say that the Jewish community should welcome every convert with warmth and enthusiasm. But the data make it clear that conversion is no antidote to the alarming demographic data revealed by the 1990 National Jewish Population Study.

The Outreach Delusion

The significance of all these data is dismissed, or at least denigrated, by those who argue that it can all be changed by "outreach." Instead of a demographic *crisis,* they say, there is a new *opportunity* for American Judaism.

This is a compelling notion, urging, as it does, that the Jewish community makes it possible for people in mixed marriages to feel welcome within it.* But it can also become a slogan, using the language of feel-good pop psychology: "Outreach empowers, enabling born Jews and Jews-by-Choice alike to own Judaism," said the director of Reform Judaism's Commission on Reform Jewish Outreach.[42] The meaning of this phrase is clear enough. Far from being an unavoidable use of scarce resources, an effort made necessary by the high intermarriage rate, outreach here becomes a goal in itself. The problem, in this view, isn't the Jew who intermarries; it's the

---

*A more extreme notion of "outreach" was proposed by Rabbi Alexander Schindler when he headed the Reform movement. In 1993 he proposed a $5 million program to seek out and convert unaffiliated non-Jews to Judaism. This initiative has not prospered, and Jewish evangelism is not now seriously proposed as a response to Jewish demographic problems.

unwillingness of a backward Jewish community to embrace the new couple and make it feel at home. And the solution isn't to stop the intermarrying, but to change the community's reaction.

Intermarriage, in other words, is an opportunity. As president of the Center for Jewish Outreach to the Intermarried in 1990, David W. Belin argued that "in our free society, the battle to stop intermarriage cannot be won. But . . . we have the capability to transform the intermarriage crisis into the greatest opportunity in modern Jewish history."[43]

If Belin evinces more enthusiasm for intermarriage than most Jews may feel, the idea behind "outreach" is simple and powerful. With half of all Jews who marry these days marrying non-Jews, and so many children growing up in mixed families, it is critically important to try to win the mixed couple and especially its children back to Judaism. To this end a variety of programs have been implemented, above all within Reform Judaism. This is natural, since Reform is more afflicted by intermarriage than Conservative or Orthodox Judaism. For the Jewish community in general, and for Reform Judaism in particular, outreach programs have been called "demographic imperatives."[44]

Outreach programs are bound to do some good for many individuals and congregations. There are unquestionably Jews and former Jews searching for a spiritual home and open to the possibility that it can be found in Judaism. Certainly many Jews have looked very far for inspiration: "the Guru of a prominent Buddhist movement once came to the United States to try to discover why a majority of his members in this country were Jewish."[45] Perhaps such people, in addition to the mixed-marriage families that are the central targets of outreach programs, can indeed be brought back.

The very least the community can do is ensure that any expression of interest in joining it—any outreach *to* it—is met with a warm and open response. This means devising programs aimed at educating the non-Jewish spouse or the children in a mixed marriage, as well as responding to the born Jew who seeks a more intimate involvement with his or her faith. To the extent that outreach shows hesitant or searching people that the Jewish community welcomes them, it can be a force for good.

But as a movement it is not so simple. To begin with, it assumes that intermarriage produces assimilation when the reverse is more likely true. But if assimilation produces intermarriage, how can one combat the underlying cause? By the time an intermarried individual is contacted by an outreach program, it will often be too late. The individual's sense of Jewishness may be too attenuated to allow for a revival.

Moreover, outreach strategies may backfire. The question of rabbinic officiation at mixed marriages raises this issue. It is often argued that the refusal of a rabbi to officiate at a mixed marriage will offend both the Jewish and gentile partners, alienating both from Judaism and imperiling later outreach efforts. Thus rabbis ought to be willing—indeed, pleased to be asked—to perform intermarriages. A related belief is that it is foolish for parents to resist the intermarriage of their children, for similar reasons.

But the data suggest the argument is misconceived, and harmful. A 1987 American Jewish Committee study of intermarriage found that the willingness of a rabbi to officiate at the wedding had no statistical impact on whether the non-Jewish partner later converted. In some cases, the rabbinic refusal conveyed the message that the only way to have a Jewish wedding was to become a Jew, and the non-Jewish partner then did so.[46] Similarly, a 1989 survey found "no connection" between rabbinic officiation at a mixed marriage and the later connections of the couple to Judaism, and concluded that "Rabbis who have justified their decisions to officiate at mixed marriages on the assumption that they were helping 'save' the couple for Judaism may wish to reconsider their position."[47]

The 1987 AJC study found that "it was the converts more than the nonconverts who had experienced most resistance, initially, particularly from the Jewish mother-in-law."[48] Similarly, earlier surveys determined that "parental attitude was significant: the Columbia study [of Jewish students at Columbia University in the 1960s] and an early-1970s national survey suggested that parents who did not strongly oppose intermarriage were much more likely to end up with intermarried children than parents who chose adamant opposition."[49] The lesson here would seem to be that resistance to intermarriage is a more effective reaction than passive acceptance of this "inevitable" phenomenon. Similarly, "Converts were more likely than nonconverts to report that their Jewish spouses were "not happy" about their Christian backgrounds, while nonconverts largely perceived the issue to have been of little concern to their partners."[50] Here again, old-fashioned attitudes about intermarriage seem to work better than more modern "outreach." When the Jewish spouse is utterly indifferent to the Jewish faith, how likely is it that an outreach program will succeed in attracting and ultimately converting the Christian spouse? It can be no surprise that a study of Reform Jews found that "those from the most observant backgrounds are much more likely to influence their born non-Jewish spouses or fiancees to convert to Judaism."[51] Religious observance worked better than "outreach."

But once a couple is married and the question is whether their children will be Jewish, outreach is the best bet, its proponents agree.

It is far from clear that this is so. First comes the question of money: outreach programs aren't free. With stretched budgets, Jewish organizations (including synagogues) must reduce here to spend there. The question then is whether outreach is really more productive than inreach. Is it more sensible to focus on unmixed Jewish families, to try to increase *their* level of religious observance and synagogue attendance? Is it more productive to zero in on children of two Jewish parents, and try with limited budgets to persuade *them* not to intermarry? A powerful case can be made that inreach ought to get preference over outreach for limited community budget dollars. As one intermarriage specialist put it in an American Jewish Committee publication,

> I do not believe that it is feasible to significantly increase the number of conversions of intermarried partners to Judaism. I do believe it is feasible to help a Jew to appreciate the richness, majesty, and wonder of Judaism so that they want to join with another Jew in transmitting those values to future generations.[52]

Then there is the problem of definition. If outreach means efforts to bring people into the synagogue in adult and child education programs, then it will be beneficial. If it means changing the borders of the Jewish community so that they suddenly include people and practices not formerly considered Jewish, that is another matter.

Nearly 90 percent of Reform temples now grant membership to non-Jewish spouses. (By contrast, the Rabbinical Assembly and the United Synagogue of the Conservative movement have ruled that non-Jews cannot be members of Conservative synagogues or be invited to read from the Torah.) Similarly, if less seriously, American delegates to the 1994 international convention of B'nai B'rith (which means "sons of the covenant") wanted to extend membership to non-Jewish spouses but were voted down by foreign delegates.[53]

How far can this point be taken? In the journal of the Reform rabbinate, red flags have already been raised. Rabbi Michael Meyer argued in 1993 that

> No issue has recently risen so steeply in the collective consciousness of Reform Judaism as has the role of non-Jews in the synagogue. . . .

Despite some opposition, one congregation after another has reached out to non-Jewish partners in mixed marriages by taking them in, not merely as welcome regular guests, but as full members, sometimes also as officers of the congregation, as religious school teachers and as ritual participants. . . . With the trend for the future clearly in the direction of an ever increasing number of mixed marriages and with such mixed couples, if they decide to affiliate, disproportionately choosing the Reform temple as their spiritual home (or as one of their spiritual homes!), the influence of persons with a directly personal link to Christianity will necessarily increase.[54]

Meyer wondered when even the new, stretched limits would be pushed further. "When will we begin to hear demands that not only should Christians be given full equality in the Reform temple but also—at least up to a point—so should Christianity?"[55] Is a lobby Christmas tree alongside the menorah, or a recitation of the Lord's Prayer by the Christian spouse during some religious ceremony in the temple, any longer unthinkable? This too is outreach. Where does it lead? Meyer warns of the possibilities.

We find ourselves on the "slippery slope" toward syncretism and sectarianism, propelled by the desire always to embrace and never to exclude. Ahead lies the prospect of a Reform Judaism . . . in which conversion has become superfluous or meaningless since it has no clearly defined goal and since nonconverts feel no estrangement whatsoever within a Reform temple that welcomes them not only as individuals who are not yet Jewish, but also as continuing adherents of a sister faith that is gaining increased status within Judaism itself.[56]

Outreach, then, is not just a simple reaction to intermarriage. It is a program fraught with choices, and dangers, as traditional limits are approached and often breached. To the degree that it is understood as a modest addition to the community's programming, it can be extremely valuable. But what of the more grandiose visions of recreating the Jewish community, or creating a new Jewish community on the ruins of an older one largely wrecked by intermarriage? As Meyer noted, there is a tension here: if the barriers to Judaism are lowered to include more people within them, the incentive to convert is reduced. When the Jewish partner stresses his Judaism, and his parents do as well, there is a better chance of conversion. When the non-Jewish spouse is welcome to participate in synagogue life as a temple official, as is the case in so many Reform temples, and when the children of the mixed marriage are already considered Jewish, have outreach efforts begun to defeat their very purpose?

Nearly thirty years ago Eugene Borowitz, the leading Reform theologian of the day, wrote that

> Clarifying Jewish faith might bring many to the conclusion that they cannot honestly participate in Judaism and the synagogue. No one wishes to lose Jews for Judaism, but the time has come when the synagogue must be saved for the religious Jew, when it must be prepared to let some Jews opt out so that those who remain in, or who come in, will not be diverted from their duty to God. As the religion of a perpetual minority, Judaism must always first be concerned with the saving remnant.[57]

Borowitz was urging that Judaism must never be remodeled to attract the largest possible number of marginal Jews. Borowitz would, of course, disagree with Conservative and Orthodox thinkers about where the borders of the "hedge" around the Jewish community should be drawn, but he is arguing as strongly as they would that they must be drawn, and without reference to outreach efforts. Non-Jews should be brought to the border between Judaism and other religions and encouraged to cross, but that border should not be moved.

In 1983 the Reform movement moved that border, accommodating those in mixed marriages in which the mother was Christian. Jewish law, *Halachah,* defines the offspring of a Jewish mother as a Jew, but the Reform movement now counts the offspring of a Jewish father as well, so long as the child manifests some attachment to the Jewish community. This has created a conflict with the Orthodox and the Conservatives, and has laid the foundation for future disagreements about the status of many offspring of mixed marriages. Now, more than a decade later, it is clear that decision sowed dissension within the Jewish world; can it be said that it has increased the vitality of Reform Judaism? An article in the Reform rabbinical journal in 1992 answered the question directly:

> why should a prospective female convert become Jewish for the sake of religious unity in the family if her children will be considered Jewish anyway? . . . The exact relationship between the onset of the patrilineality principle [1983] and its effect on conversion is unclear. It is statistically accurate that, since the inception of the principle and now, the number of intermarriages has steadily increased and the rate of conversion has slightly decreased.[58]

Clearly the Reform movement remains deeply torn on issues related to outreach. In late 1995 it issued a recommendation to member congregations stepping back from the frontiers of outreach, encouraging Hebrew schools to bar training for children of mixed marriages who were simultaneously receiving education in another religion.[59] Yet at the same time, pressure from Reform congregation members and officials for their rabbis to perform intermarriages is so strong that rabbis who refuse are finding it increasingly difficult to land jobs. One candidate reported that "the second question he was asked after 'Hello, how are you?' was 'Do you perform intermarriages?'" When he said he did not, "he was told that the interview was over."[60]

The difficulty for the Reform movement is likely to increase rather than diminish, for "the Reform rabbinate is tending more toward tradition, while the lay movement is becoming increasingly liberal to shore up its dwindling ranks," the Jewish newspaper *Forward* reported. The high rate of intermarriages has led to additional pressure for allowing more intermarriages, and for allowing a looser and looser definition of who is a Jew and what constitutes acceptable Jewish practice.

Chapter 6

THE FLIGHT FROM JUDAISM

The steady increase in intermarriage rates becomes easier to understand when we examine the present state of Jewish belief. That many American Jews fear Christianity, as we have seen, is no secret. And yet, far less acknowledged, albeit much greater in its impact on the Jewish community, is the Jews' widespread anxiety about Judaism. For if the early Jewish strategy for success in America, with its requirement of "social invisibility," might be thwarted by the actions and beliefs of Christians, it could also be thwarted by the strict ritual requirements of Judaism, and the Jews who clung to them. If Christianity is believed to be the continuing source of anti-Semitism, Judaism is thought to constitute an even more powerful potential barrier to the integration and the success of American Jews.

This is a jarring thought for most American Jews. They have devised a variety of substitutes for Judaism without consciously acknowledging that the search for alternatives to their religion is motivated not only by the desire to do good works and through them to remain Jewish, but as well by the desire to escape the constraints of a terribly demanding faith.

When Jews emerged from Europe's ghettos and began to live as part of the broader society, the very meaning of being a Jew

changed. Jews had previously lived among Christians but as a separate nation. Now they were to become fellow citizens, able to participate in social and political life, to intermarry, and to drift away
from their own religion and people without necessarily converting
to Christianity. For most eastern European Jews, these were remote
possibilities. But in western Europe they were real, and gave rise to
a redefinition of the Jew: no longer the member of a separate nation, like the Frenchman or the Greek, but solely the adherent of a
faith, like their Christian compatriots. Thus one could be a good
Jew and a loyal German or American, a citizen who happened to be
of the Jewish faith.

And in Germany, and then in America when German Jews emigrated there, that faith itself was "reformed" to make it more compatible with modern life amid a Christian majority. As Nathan
Glazer wrote, "Judaism, which had been the religion of all the Jewish people, [became] Orthodoxy, which is the position of only
some of them."[1] In fact, if reformers and modernizers of various
kinds had been in the minority among European Jews, the traditionally observant soon became the minority in America.

The Flight from Judaism

The flight from Judaism is very clear in the data about the predom-
inant Jewish beliefs and practices. The problem is not that American Jews refuse to be Orthodox, for even the term "Orthodox" is
subject to varying interpretations. Orthodoxy itself is deeply divided, the sharpest line being that between the "modern Orthodox"
who seek to live as traditional Jews within American society and
Hasidim of various sects. While the motto of Yeshiva University, a
bastion of modern Orthodoxy, is "Torah and Science," the Hasidim
withdraw from modern society and—like the Amish—avoid higher
education, live separately, dress differently, and view the modern

Orthodox as unauthentic Jews. Even if someone were to posit that Jews should be Orthodox, that would be only the beginning of the struggle; there would then be mighty battles over whose approach to traditional Judaism was "correct." There are very many divisions among Jews who consider themselves faithful to Torah and to Jewish law.

The real problem, however, is that most American Jews are not only not Orthodox, they are not Conservative or Reform either. Both of those movements have standards of behavior, such as belonging to a synagogue and attending Sabbath services, that the majority of American Jews—the unaffiliated and the self-described Conservative or Reform Jews—do not meet. "Religion is a low priority for American Jews, who lag behind the general population in membership in a congregation, worship attendance, and the importance they place on religion in their lives."[2] Thus concluded George Gallup Jr. and Joseph Castelli in their 1989 book, *The People's Religion: American Faith in the 90s.* In answer to Gallup and company's question whether religion was "very important" in their lives, Americans on average said yes 55 percent of the time, and no only 14 percent. American Jews, however, said yes only 30 percent of the time, and no 35 percent of the time.

A Gallup poll taken in December 1991 asked New Yorkers "How important is religion in your life?" The results: 74 percent of blacks, 57 percent of white Catholics, 47 percent of white Protestants, and only 34 percent of Jews said religion was "very important."[3] (And as we shall see, many of those Jews may have meant "Jewishness" rather than Judaism.)

Yet, remarkably, in an almost simultaneous study done by the American Jewish Committee, many American Jews continued to claim strong ties to their community, with 70 percent reporting some organizational affiliation, and 65 percent reporting that they were satisfied with their level of involvement. What makes these claims so remarkable is that the figures apply to a phantom affiliation. A majority of that group had paid no dues or membership fees to any Jewish organization, and what's more had attended none of their meetings. That is the level of involvement with their community organizations that most Jews found fully satisfactory.[4]

And if religion is less important to Jews than to their non-Jewish neighbors, it may also mean something different to Jews. In a 1989 American Jewish Committee survey, 81 percent of Jews responded that it was very important that their children feel good about being Jewish, but only 46 percent said it was important that they practice Jewish rituals. Ninety percent "agreed or agreed strongly" that "a Jew can be religious even if he or she isn't particularly observant." Seventy-two percent said God was very important as a symbol or concept in their sense of being Jewish, while 78 percent said "American anti-Semitism" was, 79 percent said the High Holidays were, and 85 percent said the Holocaust was.[5] Among Reform Jewish leaders, 44 percent said a person could be a good Jew without believing in God at all.[6] When a *Los Angeles Times* survey in 1988 asked "what do you consider most important to your Jewish identity?," 17 percent of respondents said "religious observance," while 59 percent answered "a commitment to social justice."[7]

And if the basic elements of religiosity—faith and practice—are of less and less importance to most Jews as time goes by, so, too, is synagogue affiliation. In the 1990s only about 40 percent of Jewish households report that they contain someone who is a synagogue member—and that low figure may be too high, for individuals sometimes report that they are members of a synagogue they once belonged to or sometimes visit. But even granting the accuracy of that figure, the majority of Jewish households have not one person in them who even belongs to a synagogue—let alone attends one.

Among fourth-generation Jews (those whose great-grandparents were immigrants) 8 percent of Conservative Jews and 2.5 percent of Reform Jews attend once a month or more.[8] By comparison, Gallup recently found that 67 percent of Americans belong to a religious institution and 58 percent attend once a month or more.[9]

To be a Jew in America, indeed to be a good Jew, did not and does not to most American Jews require traditional ritual observance: it no longer means praying three times daily, studying the Torah, keeping kosher, and respecting the Sabbath. Instead, it means feeling oneself a part of the "Jewish community," giving money to that community's institutions, and supporting the liberal and secularist prescriptions for American society that would theoretically allow American Jews to thrive. The perceived interests of the community, and the act of working to advance those interests, have been sacralized, and have became a sort of secular religion themselves. A model Jew in America is not off in the synagogue at prayer but out at a meeting discussing a new hospital, a trip to Israel, or a new fund-raising drive.

Here, as Glazer put it in his famous work, *American Judaism,* the community's

> focus would not be religion but something we may call "Jewishness," which would be the common element in a variety of activities—religious, political, cultural, intellectual, philanthropic, all of them legitimately Jewish. This type of community, it was hoped, would replace the dying East European Orthodoxy and maintain Judaism in a new form adapted to America.[10]

Jewish leaders—whether the rich German Jews who founded most of the old American Jewish institutions or the professionals who staffed those agencies—after all wanted their community to survive in America, not to disappear. Similarly, the masses of immigrant Jews and their children who left Orthodoxy, or embraced the secularist ideal, sought to accommodate to life in America, so that they could in some sense live as Jews here—not so that they could abandon entirely any trace of Jewish connections. In this they were all of one mind.

The earliest Jewish organizations in America had been religious in the narrowest sense: synagogues, burial societies, cemeteries. A new pattern arose after the German Jewish emigration of the 1840s, and B'nai B'rith, for example, was founded in 1843 to concern itself with the lives, not the souls, of Jews in America. By 1900, "the synagogue had lost its place as the center of communal life, and had been supplanted by a network of institutions, philanthropic and educational, which now commanded first place."[11] The American Jewish Committee, for example, was founded in 1906 to speak for the Jewish community on public policy issues, defend American and foreign Jews, and help the new immigrants become at home in America. The Anti-Defamation League was founded in 1913, to fight anti-Semitism.

Both the nature of the work these institutions engaged in and their constant need for fund-raising reinforced the leadership of wealthier (and usually more secular) Jewish elites over that of religious authorities. As was discussed in Chapter Two, they were run, at least until after World War II, by a self-perpetuating and self-appointed group of wealthy, assimilated, usually German Jews like Louis Marshall (the New York lawyer who was the first president of the American Jewish Committee), Jacob Schiff (the Wall Street banker and one of the richest Jews in America), and Louis Brandeis (the Boston lawyer who became the first Jewish member of the Supreme Court).

These leaders tried to organize help for a community consisting mostly, by the time of World War I, of poor eastern European Jews to survive in and adapt to America. Their organizations provided everything from medical clinics, to courses in English, to care for widows and orphans. No doubt their motivations included self-interest and self-defense, for they believed that if those urban Jewish masses did not adapt, becoming less separate and less visible, the anti-Semitism that might well result could threaten every Jew in America. They did not want those immigrants on the public dole, much less in the police dockets. Nor did they want them all concentrated in just a few East Coast cities, and they made efforts to send immigrant Jews to the Middle West to try farming. And no doubt they often looked down their noses at these poor and uncultured immigrants; the president of B'nai B'rith in 1906 opposed elections to choose leaders of the American Jewish Committee, asking if it were "necessary that this Committee represents the riff raff" instead of just "the high class Jews of America."[12]

Whatever else the Jewish elites felt, they acted also out of a feeling of obligation and of solidarity. Most of them would have said they acted to help coreligionists, new Americans of the Hebrew faith, rather than out of common ethnicity, race, or nationhood. Still, they acted as Jews, and evinced no more desire to escape from that condition than did the recipients of their largesse. But among the things they provided to the new arrivals, along with their charitable donations, was an ideology, and it was not only non-Orthodox but secularist. By their own conduct and by the positions they advanced in the organizations they led, they offered the community a new understanding of the meaning of being a Jew.

The "Civil Religion" of American Jews

No one has better analyzed this change than Jonathan Woocher in his book *Sacred Survival,* where he describes the set of beliefs that came to replace traditional Judaism as the new "civil religion" of American Jews. The life of this new religion is carried on not in synagogues but in the "vast array" of community organizations, originally the B'nai B'rith and the American Jewish Committee and now including the Federations of Jewish Philanthropies and the Jewish Community Relations Councils.

These philanthropic activities became not additions to American Judaism but the very substance of it. *Tzedakah,* a word whose direct meaning is righteousness, came to signify above all charity, and many Jews came to believe that charity was itself the heart of the Jewish religion.[13] Philanthropy, the Harvard historian Oscar Handlin wrote, "was important not only for what it actually accomplished, but because it was the means by which [American Jews] engaged in communal endeavors. . . . philanthropy came to express the meaning of 'Jewishness.'"[14] For many Jews, then, philanthropy became their religion, with its own rituals and commandments. Religion per se could be divisive, even within the community, split as it was among Orthodox, Conservative, and Reform Jews. But philanthropy could unite all elements of the community, and the good works being accomplished seemed beyond controversy. Philanthropic activity was sacralized, transformed from good citizenship into a religious obligation and a religious act. It achieved transcendent significance.[15] The result was a miracle of fund-raising successes that became a model for other ethnic communities and a byword for philanthropic achievement. In their ability to reach very high percentages of American Jews, in the ever-increasing amounts of dollars they raised, and in their effective expenditure of those sums, Jewish charities and community organizations in America were legendary.

The good works achieved by the American Jewish civic organizations have been immense, but the demographic crisis of American Jewry shows that they have failed to keep American Jews Jewish. Civil Judaism is a faith that—unlike Judaism—is apparently very difficult to transmit from one generation to the next. How can one judge? One indicator is the age of the membership in several of the major Jewish organizations, for a high average suggests that as long-time members age, new and younger members are not joining. The average age of American women is thirty-seven, but the average member of the leading women's Zionist organization, Hadassah, is fifty-four. Thirty percent of American Jewish women are under thirty-four years of age, but only 5.5 percent of Hadassah members are.[16] Even more striking are the numbers for the fraternal organization B'nai B'rith, whose members have an average age of sixty-five.[17] In effect, as the old members get older, their children are not joining these organizations.

Nor are Hadassah and B'nai B'rith unique. Herbert Friedman, the chief executive of United Jewish Appeal from 1955 to 1975, wrote in 1991 that "the reality is that in recent years the organization has lost the confidence of many Jews."[18] This is reflected in patterns of donations, and the share of philanthropic giving that many major donors direct toward their Jewish charities is falling.[19] UJA/Federation now receives 25–30 percent of the total charitable contributions of many major donors, down from 70 percent only a few years ago.[20] Gary Tobin of Brandeis found that younger Jews give a smaller proportion of their charitable gifts to Jewish organizations, and concluded that "[a]s a form of involvement, the current fundraising systems, especially the [United Jewish Appeal/United Israel Appeal], have failed to engage most Jews in a serious way. The data indicate that some older Jews used to contribute but no longer do, and that most younger Jews have never contributed."[21]

Why not? Civil Judaism can provide the mechanisms for doing good works for fellow Jews, but it cannot provide a motivation. Why not contribute time and money to the museum or symphony instead of the local Federation of Jewish Philanthropies? Often an emotional answer (immigrant parents, old neighborhoods, child-hood associations) suffices for the long-time donor or activist, but it seems less and less to suffice for the donor's children and grand-children.

Many of the major Jewish organizations reacted to the 1990 National Jewish Population Study, and to the data showing declining support in younger generations, by addressing this problem head-on with new programs stressing "continuity." If the problem was that younger generations were leaving the Jewish community, the Jewish agencies would now focus on keeping them. Even organizations like the American Jewish Committee, American Jewish Congress, and the Jewish Labor Committee, secular institutions never before involved with Jewish continuity, have begun to talk this language. This means that much new information has become available, as groups try to study "what works" in keeping Jews Jewish. Moreover, many new programs have undoubtedly had some positive effects, at the very least in shifting attention to the crisis the Jewish community is facing.

One may question whether all these institutions are well fitted to address the continuity issue. Communitywide "continuity" programs virtually guarantee that scarce funding will be spread very wide, and spent on some institutions whose contributions to this new agenda cannot be large—such as the agencies whose traditional work is defense against anti-Semitism or "community relations" among ethnic groups.

The ability of the major Jewish secular agencies to deal with the continuity agenda is doubted even by their own supporters. When one researcher asked Jewish donors if they would raise their contributions to fund "continuity" programs, they said no: "Individuals did not indicate that they would give much more to develop programs to prevent assimilation, even though they believe this is the number one problem facing the Jewish community in the United States today. This reluctance came largely from a disbelief that such programs could be developed."[22]

The disbelief is well founded, for "continuity" cannot in itself justify these institutions' existence. As a goal, it is subject to the challenge "why bother?" and these secular institutions cannot answer that question. Something is absent from the picture, and Jonathan Woocher puts the matter plainly.

> There is one notable element of traditional religion conspicuously missing from the picture of civil Judaism which we have drawn thus far: reference to G-d, or some form of transcendent reality. . . . What is most striking . . . is the thoroughly insignificant role which any G-d-concept plays in the civil religion.[23]

In fact, continuity as a goal can turn the purpose of Jewish life on its head. It risks making everything else, including Judaism, seem to be but a tool of Jewish continuity, when in truth continuity itself is valuable only if it serves the survival of Judaism. "Continuity" risks confusing the means and ends of Jewish existence.

Moreover, continuity programs cannot work unless they are centered on faith in God. The civil religion cannot reliably be passed from generation to generation. This conclusion has already been reached, privately, by increasing numbers of the people who work in the major Jewish organizations. These organizations were largely staffed in the past by secular, often left-wing personnel with a negative attitude toward religion.[24] But today the staff people are often far more religious than the American Jewish community as a whole. Graduates of Jewish day schools form a high percentage of the staffs of more and more Jewish communal organizations, producing an enormous cultural change within them.[25] Daniel Elazar explained it in 1990:

> Today, Jewish communal service, like the rabbinate or Jewish education, attracts those who are committed to Judaism in all its facets and who find a Jewish career environment makes life richer for them as

135

observant Jews. We do not have percentages available, but the change is palpable, especially among the younger age groups. . . . The non-Orthodox on the federation staffs are drawn increasingly from among the serious Conservative Jews, whose personal and family observance level is high."[26]

Thus more and more of the professionals responsible for institutional programming recognize that it can address only one part of the current problem—the easy part—by adopting specifically targeted new continuity programs. Such programming may acknowledge that today's American Jewish community is remarkably ignorant of Jewish history and tradition and is highly nonobservant. It may result in new educational initiatives, new commitments to Hillel student organizations (the B'nai B'rith's campus arm), and various efforts to head off intermarriage ranging from lectures against it to "mixers" that bring marriage-age Jews together. All these programs are helpful, but more and more of the people who run them appear to believe that strong and permanent Jewish identity comes from only one source: faith in God. They appear to believe that, absent strong religious faith, American Jews will be pursuing what has rightly been called "continuity without content."[27] In their own lives, increasing numbers of those who staff the Jewish agencies do not depend on agency activities to guarantee Jewish continuity; they turn to Judaism for that purpose.

Jewish community activism does not sustain Judaism in America, but the converse is true: Judaism does sustain community institutions. The National Jewish Population Survey of 1990 and other studies show "a direct relationship between religious commitment and support for Jewish communal institutions. . . . identification with Judaism is the critical variable for Jewish continuity in America. . . . The health of American Judaism thus has a direct impact on the viability and unity of the Jewish people in America."[28]

The future of the secular institutions depends on the future of Jewish religious life in America, not vice versa. For decades these secular institutions—the American Jewish Committee and Congress, the Anti-Defamation League, the Community Relations Councils, and the Federations—have been the heart of Jewish community life. What Jews did in the public square was considered more significant than what happened in homes and synagogues. But it turns out that the future depends on what Jews do in private. And that will be determined by their commitment to Judaism, not their stance on public policy issues.

The Religion of Israel

If philanthropy and good works replaced Judaism as the faith of many American Jews, support for the state of Israel came to be the faith of even more. Indeed, it is not too much to say that support for Israel became the key element of Jewish faith for most American Jews.

Support for Israel became central to Jewish identity—"the core of the religion of American Jews."[29] To many American Jews, it became the essence of their lives as Jews and of their understanding of their own Jewishness. They loved Israel, and they supported Israel. A good Jew could do no less, and one who did no less—*and no more*—was a good Jew.

A myriad of Jewish organizations and events connect American Jews to the state of Israel, and themes relating to Israel are absolutely pervasive in Jewish public discourse. There can be no doubt that, as much as American Jews have done for Israel, Israel has done a very great deal for American Jewry in return. Many American Jews who have no other connection to the community or to Judaism have rallied to the cause of Israel.

It had not always been so, and there was a long debate among European and American Jews over Zionism. Jews had prayed for a return to Zion since their defeat and expulsion by Rome in the year 70 C.E., and the Passover seder, or dinner, ended with the phrase "Next Year in Jerusalem." But Zionism as an active political movement was a creature of the late nineteenth century. Despite the post-Enlightenment, post-French Revolution political and social progress in Europe, the plight of the Jews at the hands of their Christian neighbors and rulers did not improve. From the wave of bloody pogroms in Russia beginning in 1881, to the Dreyfus case in France (where anti-Semitism led to the unjust conviction for treason of a Jewish army officer), it seemed that the "Jewish question" in Europe was no nearer a solution. Some Jews came to believe that the entire social and economic system must change, and they became Socialists; some simply emigrated to America; but others began to argue that the Jews could solve their own problems if they had a land of their own. In the last two decades of the century, twenty-five thousand Jews actually left Europe to live in Palestine. Modern Zionism as a movement is usually traced to Theodore Herzl and his 1896 book, *The Jewish State,* where he explained that the Jews' problem was that they were a people without a state. Safety and survival would be achieved when a Jewish state came into existence.

Zionism as a nineteenth- and early-twentieth-century political movement thus sought a homeland for the Jews, to which they could escape from exile and oppression in the diaspora; this was Theodore Herzl's main goal for the movement he founded. Yet Zionism was not merely political: it had as well religious and cultural goals (although not all Zionists shared these), both to reinvigorate Judaism everywhere and to fulfill God's pledges by restoring the Promised Land to the people to whom it had been promised. Zionism was, in this latter view, a form of nationalism inherent in the spiritual heritage of every Jew.[30] It was—and is—

an answer to the question, How should a Jew live? The Zionist answer was, and is, a Jew should live in the land of Israel. This notion seemed self-evident to many Jews in Europe but heretical to others, who said it contradicted the belief that God would send the Messiah and return His people to Zion when he was ready.

But in America the terms of the argument were different. The problem was illustrated when an American delegate to the First Zionist Congress told Herzl that Zionism only meant providing a home for Jews who were homeless. Herzl replied, "All Jews have homes, and yet they are all homeless."[31] American Jews did not view themselves this way, and indeed many agreed with what an American rabbi said in the early part of the nineteenth century: "America is our Zion and Washington our Jerusalem."[32] Of what, then, did American "Zionism" consist? How could Zionism appeal to American Jews, who had already found safety and religious freedom in the New World, and who worried lest their loyalty and patriotism be challenged?

The opposition to Zionism was especially strong in the Reform movement, which took prayers for a return to Zion out of its liturgy. Rabbi Kaufmann Kohler, who rose to head the Reform movement's rabbinical college, called the traditional prayers for a return to Jerusalem "a blasphemy and a lie upon the lips of every American Jew."[33] At the close of the nineteenth century the leader of Reform Judaism, Rabbi Isaac Mayer Wise, proclaimed that "the Jews do not want Palestine. The Jews who are in Palestine are the lowest of their class, as a rule; bodies of paupers sustained by gifts, otherwise unable to survive."[34] Jews would not leave modern western countries "to form a ridiculous miniature state in dried up Palestine," Wise wrote after Theodore Herzl's First Zionist Congress in 1897.[35] The (Reform) Union of American Hebrew Congregations, which in 1898 had claimed that "America is our Zion," did not move away from its strong anti-Zionist leanings until 1947, when it adopted a generally positive—not fervently Zionist—position.[36]

Outside the Reform movement, American Jews were divided about Zionism. The German Jewish elites were split; Louis Brandeis became the leader of the American Zionist movement, but many others saw the movement as unpatriotic. The notion that American Jews had a homeland elsewhere to which they might owe any loyalty was anathema to those who viewed equality and social integration in America as the community's true goal. Charity toward Jews who lived in the Holy Land was one thing, but the argument that there lay the homeland of all Jews was quite another, and it was rejected, before World War II, by most of the richest American Jews. Among the Yiddish-speaking immigrants from eastern Europe, however, there was always great support for the movement. They viewed Zionism not as an ideology but as an expression of Jewish solidarity and as a possible help to the Jews who were still in Europe.

The debate raged with passion for decades, with Zionist and anti-Zionist forces present among Socialist, Orthodox, and Reform leaders. But the view that emerged entirely victorious was the one delineated initially by the premier American Zionist leader of the early twentieth century, Justice Brandeis. The essence of American Zionism was "practical work" to build a Jewish homeland in Zion—not religious or cultural revival, not Jewish national unity. "It is democracy that Zionism represents. It is Social Justice which Zionism represents," he said in 1915, choosing terms that stressed the compatibility of the movement with Americanism.[37] There is nothing here of mystic national ties or of redemption. If Chaim Weizmann, after Herzl the premier Zionist leader in the West, saw Zionism as a movement aimed at awakening the entire Jewish people, Brandeis saw it as a pragmatic program to rebuild a Jewish presence in Palestine. And Brandeis' view, not that of the cultural or religious Zionists, came to dominate American Jewish thinking. Zionism became "little more than a philanthropic endeavor."[38]

That philanthropy became critically important, for soon there was much "practical work" to be done. When the doors of the United States and of western Europe's democracies were closed to Jews while anti-Semitism in Europe exploded in the 1930s, a safe haven for them in Palestine became a critical goal. American Zionism then meant sustaining the Jewish settlements in Palestine, seeking access to the area as a haven for Jewish refugees fleeing Hitler, and at least in principle supporting the goal of a Jewish state.

That safe haven was not provided, and the result was the death of untold numbers of Jews who might otherwise have escaped the Holocaust. For the American Jewish community this clinched the case for Zionism, at least as American Jews by then understood that concept. The Jewish state would be a haven for Jews in the future, and would instantly provide a home for the Jews who were then in displaced persons camps in Europe.

And once the state was in fact established, the experience of the Holocaust gave special strength to the desire to support and defend it, for defending it meant protecting the lives of that remnant of European Jewry that had survived Hitler. Now that a Jewish state existed, it had a claim on the heart of most American Jews simply because danger to the state meant danger to fellow Jews.

This became clear in 1967, when war seemed to threaten the very survival of Israel. That survival had not been threatened in 1956, during the Suez War, but 1967 saw an Arab attack with every hope of victory. If we recall today Israel's victory in what came to be known as the Six-Day War, after Egyptian President Nasser closed the Suez Canal to Israel, the international community refused to react, and Israel seemed to stand absolutely alone before the combined Arab threat—we may find it difficult to understand the mounting anxiety among American Jews in June 1967. It seemed, once again, that the world might stand by and watch while Jews were attacked and slaughtered. For the first time since World War II ended, American Jews were forced to contemplate the possibility of another immense Jewish tragedy.

They reacted with an emotional outpouring of support for Israel from all quarters of the organized community—and from unaffiliated Jews whose reaction surprised even themselves. The 1967 War transformed what had been solid support into a faith that must be called religious, and that provided a center to the beliefs and activities of millions of American Jews. Jews spoke of the "eleventh commandment"—no posthumous victories for Hitler—and faced with a possible new Holocaust found their hearts moved. The passionate commitment to Israel must be dated not to 1948 but 1967. Leonard Fein wrote that

> for very many Jews, the experience of the Six Day War had religious significance. Specifically, it was after the Six Day War that Israel came to occupy the center of the Jewish religious consciousness and consensus. In a very precise way, Israel had now become the faith of the American Jew. . . . Israel has become for us a binding Jewish cement, a powerful explanation of the Jewish connection.[39]

Yet one may question whether that cement will prove to be permanent, and in fact there is evidence that it is already losing strength.

First, the American Jewish sentiment about Israel grew as the risks to Israel grew, reaching its highest and most intense levels as a result of the 1967 and 1973 wars. It is in that sense a commitment to the survival of Israel-in-danger; it is more properly denominated pro-Israelism than Zionism. As it today far exceeds the level of support that Israel enjoyed prior to 1948 or from 1948 to 1967, perhaps it exceeds the level Israel will enjoy in the future if American Jews conclude that Middle East peace efforts have greatly diminished the threat to its security. In that event, the intensity of concern about Israel-in-danger, and its centrality to the Jewishness of many American Jews, may well fade.

Moreover, American Jewish support for Israel has been, at least in part, charity from the world's largest and wealthiest Jewish community toward the needy Jewish state. It is still more "practical work." One may well question whether this cause will maintain its hold on American Jews as Israel changes—from impoverished settlements in pre-Israel Palestine under the British mandate, to a new and beleaguered land desperately trying to organize its economy, to a prosperous nation living at European levels of comfort with a per capita GDP of $13,000.

And the Israeli Jewish community no longer consists of small pioneer settlements that require alms from the much larger American Jewish population. In fact, it will not be long—perhaps fifteen years—until there are more Jews in Israel than in America, and perhaps a quarter century after that than in the rest of the world put together.[40] Israel will at that point unquestionably be the leading Jewish community in the world. This is the position that the American Jewish community has occupied at least since the rise of the Nazis destroyed the Jews of Germany, and perhaps since the start of the twentieth century. But when there are more Jews in Israel than in America, and soon thereafter than in all the rest of the world, charity is less and less likely to hold these communities together—unless it be charity from Israel to beleaguered or declining Jewish communities in the Diaspora.

With the demise of the concept of "exile," American Zionists tore the spiritual heart out of Zionism, and the pallid version that exists in the United States bears little relation to the fervent commitment that once drove Israel's founders. Perhaps American Zionism is a popular faith in part because most of its adherents find it to be that happy combination: extremely fulfilling yet equally undemanding. In fact, despite the apparently passionate concern for

143

Israel of American Jews, only about one in three has ever set foot there.[41] How likely is it that Israel can hold Jews to a commitment to Jewishness they would otherwise abandon, yet cannot even attract them for a brief visit?

A 1989 survey for the American Jewish Committee by Steven Cohen of the Hebrew University concluded that Israel was now only a "secondary concern" for American Jews. "However one looks at the matter," Cohen wrote, "caring about Israel is important to American Jews, but not all that important." Cohen found, for example, that while 61 percent of American Jews said that "to a great extent" they felt close to other American Jews, and 40 percent said they felt that close to non-Jewish Americans, only 1 percent felt equally close to Israelis. On the contrary, 23 percent said they felt "not at all" close to them.[42] A study by Gary Tobin of Brandeis University revealed that feelings about Israel are becoming "increasingly ambivalent and tenuous" among American Jews, and that while "Israel is still the single most important motivation for giving to Jewish philanthropies . . . these emotional ties are weakening, especially among the younger generations."[43]

Too often, the only form of "involvement" with Israel is writing a check or asking others to write theirs. And smaller checks are being written. A great debate has begun over what portion of Jewish charitable funds should go to Israel and how much be kept at home. The trend toward reducing the percentage that goes to Israel is very clear. In Boston the proportion going to Israel has been reduced from 44 to 34 percent in the last few years; in Los Angeles the percentage fell from 46 to 37 in the early 1990s; and smaller percentage reductions have been seen in such diverse communities as Milwaukee, Indianapolis, and Detroit.[44]

The powerful Jewish institutions continue their work in support of Israel, and threats to that nation continue to worry American Jews. But what is the impact of all that on the private lives of

American Jews? As Steven Bayme of the American Jewish Committee said in 1991, "Israel represents the public agenda of American Jews. However, that public agenda is perhaps the least important aspect of insuring Jewish continuity."[45]

Where is it possible to find a group of Jews who are committed to Israel, and whose children are the most likely to honor that commitment? The answer is, in a synagogue on the Sabbath. The faith of religious Jews, of whatever denomination, holds them in a permanent covenant with God and with the land of Israel and its people. Their commitment will not weaken if the Israeli government pursues unpopular policies, or if the cultural links between American and Israeli Jews attenuate. It will not decline if talk of peace, or the reality of peace, erodes the intensity of American Jewish fears about the survival of Israel as they arose after the 1967 War.

Faith is the only ultimately reliable bond between American Jews and Israel. The relationship between faith and attitudes toward Israel can even be demonstrated with survey data. Steven Cohen, in his book *American Modernity and Jewish Identity,* reported that "pro-Israelism indices are closely related to ritual observance. 'Observant' respondents are at least 25 percentage points more likely to score high on a 'pro-Israel' index than are 'secular' respondents."[46] Among young American Jews, Charles Liebman found, "the more ritually observant were more pro-Israel."[47]

In time, ties based on history and memory will fade, and charity based on the perception of a vibrant American Jewish community and Israeli weakness and vulnerability will be increasingly discordant with reality. Even the fear for Israel's safety and survival will diminish if American Jews conclude that peace is truly spreading in the Middle East. What will be left then is the covenant with God that created, and that sustains, the Jewish people and ties them to the land of Israel—or nothing.

"Prophetic Judaism" and the Religion of Politics

This is precisely the problem with "prophetic Judaism" and the link between Jewishness and politics. Most American Jews have come to believe that there is a very close relationship between Judaism and "social justice." The "prophetic tradition" in Judaism, in this view, is as much at the heart of the religion as Halachah—rabbinic law—or prayer. There is no doubt that Judaism is a "this worldly" religion, not given to postponing better days for the afterlife. But many Jews have read a great deal too much into the idea of the "prophetic tradition," virtually identifying it with the program of American liberalism and with support for the Democratic Party. In congressional elections since 1980, Jews have cast 74 percent of their votes for Democratic candidates (vs. 53 percent for the electorate at large), and gave 80 percent of their votes in 1992 to Bill Clinton, the Democratic candidate for president (while he received only 43 percent of all votes cast). In 1996, when Clinton received 49 percent of all votes cast, preliminary analyses concluded that he had received 78 percent of the votes cast by Jews. While it is sometimes argued that Jewish support for liberal candidates is diminishing, Jews remains far more liberal than non-Jews.[48]

Before the mass immigration from eastern Europe, the American Jewish community had not been notably progressive on issues unrelated to direct Jewish interests. Its leadership, drawn from its most prosperous ranks, was not particularly liberal. The Pittsburgh Platform, the famous Reform statement of principles of 1885, largely ignored political and social issues. It was in reaction to the "Social Gospel" movement that arose in Protestant denominations and to the Progressive Movement in American politics in the last decade of the 19th and first two decades of the 20th century that Reform Jews began their alignment with liberalism.[49]

But very many of eastern European Jewish immigrants were on the left politically. For poor immigrant Jews, their status as urban laborers added immediate self-interest to the philosophical attractions of socialism, trade union activism, and Democratic Party liberalism. Liberalism, wrote Steven Cohen, can be understood as the "politics of integration," the goal being the creation of an American society hospitable to Jews—and especially to poor immigrant Jews.[50] This outlook still prevails in many parts of the American Jewish community. In 1989, for example, American Jewish Committee Executive Vice President Ira Silverman said despite "a strong rightward tide of American public opinion and governmental policies," American Jews should "defy the undertow and stay rooted to the liberalism which will help ensure American pluralism and social fairness, good for us and for all Americans."[51]

For decades Silverman's view was typical of most of the key staff people in the main Jewish organizations. Though this has changed in recent years, staff people tended not only to be secular rather than religiously observant themselves but also to be on the left politically. Daniel Elazar wrote in 1976 that "what is notable about Jewish communal workers as a group is that so many of them came from relatively left-wing backgrounds. They originally entered the social-work field out of a desire to improve society."[52] An America without poverty, prejudice, or racial and religious discrimination would solve the specific problems they tackled in the Jewish agencies, and create a better milieu for the Jews in America. So their commitment was not primarily to Judaism but to social reform, or as they might have put it, to a Jewishness defined by this fight for a better America.

Yet liberalism was more than a pragmatic choice for a community of immigrants. It was widely seen, in the words of one key Reform official, as "the essence of religion, certainly of the Jewish religion."[53] The old liturgy and the rituals were marginal and outdated, "vestigial trappings."[54] Often this view is portrayed as an

147

embrace of "prophetic Judaism" as opposed to "rabbinic Judaism." The heart of prophetic Judaism is social activism and social reform—*tikkun olam,* or healing the world, in the phrase (borrowed from the *Aleinu,* the closing prayer at most Jewish services) favored by many Jewish liberals and popularized—and, some would say, corrupted—by Michael Lerner in his magazine *Tikkun.*

A poll taken in the 1960s asked Jews to rank essential qualities of being "a good Jew." Sixty-seven percent said "Support all humanitarian causes," 67 percent said "Promote civic betterment and improvement in the community," 58 percent said "help the underprivileged improve their lot," and only 48 percent said "Know the fundamentals of Judaism."[55] So liberal politics came, for many Jews, to be the heart of their Jewish identity. "For many American Jews," Steven Cohen wrote in 1983, "politics—in particular pro-Israel and liberal activity—have come to constitute their principal working definition of Jewishness. In this sense modern Jewish political movements have served as functional alternatives to conventional religion."[56]

Adherence to secular Judaism and the investment of liberal politics with sacred value are most advanced among Reform Jews, nearly half of whose leadership believe one can be a good Jew without believing in God.[57] As Frieda Kerner Furman wrote in *Beyond Yiddishkeit,* where she took a detailed look at one Reform congregation, Reform Jewish ideology "places ethics at the heart of Judaism," replacing the "ritual prescriptions of traditional Judaism." "Clearly," she noted, "liberalism and social activism stand at the heart of these views of Judaism. . . . It is interesting to observe the almost complete identification between Judaism and modern liberalism in the consciousness of many members" of the Reform temple she studied.[58]

This is true not just among Reform Jews but in the broader Jewish community as well. The 1991 American Jewish Year Book reported that at what was then the most recent annual convention of the National Jewish Community Relations Advisory Council (NJCRAC), a national umbrella organization linking hundreds of local organizations, "of all the items addressed in the Joint Program Plan, it was abortion rights that ignited the greatest enthusiasm among large numbers of Jews—apart from the Orthodox."[59] In the 1980s, a wide array of Jewish groups (including the Synagogue Council of America, which represents Orthodox and Conservative as well as Reform congregations) joined the Nuclear Freeze movement.[60] A 1988 Los Angeles Times telephone survey asked Jews in that city which among three qualities did respondents "consider most important to your Jewish identity": social justice, Israel, or religious observance. Fifty-nine percent answered "a commitment to social justice" while 17 percent chose "support for Israel" or "religious observance."[61]

It is therefore not entirely surprising that the 1994–95 NJCRAC "Joint Program Plan" includes the following goals: a national health care plan with coverage far more comprehensive than President Clinton had proposed, complete opposition to capital punishment, a strong statement about "gay rights," and a call to give the Environmental Protection Agency cabinet rank. These matters the NJCRAC—which includes 117 local and 13 national Jewish agencies—defined not as standard liberal fare but as *Jewish* interests.[62]

In its premiere issue, the editors of *Tikkun* made their contribution to this debate. The journal had been founded, in fact, by politically liberal Jews who thought the mainstream Jewish organizations were too much part of the "Establishment" and too little dedicated to social change. The new magazine would promote the view that *tikkun olam* was at the center of Judaism. "The universalistic dream of a transformation and healing of the world, the belief that peace and justice are not meant for heaven but are this-worldly necessities that must be fought for, is the particularistic cultural and religious tradition of the Jews," editor Michael Lerner wrote.[63] Later, in his book *Jewish Renewal: A Path to Healing and Transformation,* Lerner, a long-time leftist activist, suggested that the answer to the problems of the American Jewish community is more politics. He wishes, for example, to see the ancient rules of *kashrut,* determining which foods may be eaten and which are forbidden, amended to "add a new code of eco-kosher practices" based on the goals of the ecology movement. The Passover seder, he says, must be used "not just to talk about the good-old days, but to become actively engaged ourselves in planning how to transform the world. Passover seders should have this element of strategic focus—it's not just a ritual, it's an occasion to move forward the collective discussion about the strategy we are going to use to defeat the contemporary embodiments and successors to Roman imperialism." The harvest holiday of Sukkot becomes "the time the community gathers to make concrete assessments of current ecological struggles, and develops strategies for how to strengthen ecological movements in the coming year."

And Sabbath morning services, too, must include a political meeting. "Jewish renewal does not accept the notion that the week's political events are somehow irrelevant or a distraction from Shabbat services. While specific political organizing strategies tend to be avoided because of the anxiety that would be provoked by having to debate them out, more theoretical analyses of contemporary situations are encouraged. The two things that are never ruled out of a Jewish-renewal community are God and politics."[64] But Lerner's approach ensures that politics will be "ruled in" a great deal more frequently than God, since an infusion of politics rather than faith is what distinguishes his recommendations for "Jewish Renewal."

The idea that secular Judaism is true to Judaic tradition in placing the search for social justice at the center of the religion can, in any event, easily be challenged. As Jerold Auerbach argued in *Rabbis and Lawyers,* that view was part of the "search for compatibility between Judaism and Americanism." "How tempting to assume," he wrote, "that the Hebrew Bible was a preliminary draft of the American Constitution, that the Hebrew prophets were the founding fathers of American liberalism." But this compatibility thesis was deeply flawed, for "the constitutional community rests upon a conception of individual freedom, but the Torah community imposes a collective obligation of obedience."[65] Judaism is based on divine authority, not majority rule, Auerbach reminds us, and to the ancient prophets, "Justice meant nothing less than obedience to divine law."[66]

And as for the prophetic tradition, Auerbach complained that too many Americans Jews "hear in prophecy what they want to hear."[67] They do not hear the prophetic call to return to faith in God and adherence to sacred law, to *Halachah.* "Prophecy, in its time a desperate cry to return to the ancient faith of covenantal obligation, became in the modern era an exit from faith." Jews have wittingly or not "transformed prophecy into a repudiation of the very sacred-law tradition at its core."[68] In fact, the belief that Hebrew prophecy can best be appreciated if it is detached from *Halachah,* is actually closer to older Christian views of Judaism (as too legalistic and formalistic) than to the Jewish view. This idea of prophetic Judaism is a nineteenth-century construct, offered to provide an "ancient" basis for a very new view of what the Jewish religion means. The transcendent, the divine, the holy were set aside, their place taken by an Enlightenment faith in the perfectibility of man and his world.

This politicized, left-wing Judaism will not work *even on its own terms:* as the demographic and other data show, it cannot maintain the loyalties of Jews over the generations. At a recent meeting of Jewish Community Relations Council executives, the then head of the Des Moines, Iowa, Council, Ted Lapkin, explained why:

The current state of American Jewry shows rather conclusively that the "social justice" dynamic alone has abjectly failed to provide a sufficiently compelling reason for many of our brothers and sisters to maintain their sense of Jewish identity. After all, there are a plethora of secular or non-Jewish organizations which do excellent work in the social justice realm. If a person believes that striving towards social justice and Tikkun Olam constitute the primary theme of Judaism, such an individual can express his or her "Jewishness" in a completely non-Jewish organization or environment. I would submit that this line of thought has contributed to the trend which has brought American Jewry to the brink of demographic disaster.[69]

Secular Judaism, and the substitution of politics for Jewish ritual, cannot revive Jewish life in America because they remove precisely that which binds Jews together—and cannot replace it. Jewish faith and Jewish ritual sustain the Jewish community *both* by giving Jews common values and practices *and* by separating them from others—in this country, Christians—who believe different things and worship in a different way. The replacement of that which unites Jews, and separates them from Christians, by political activities that non-Jews can undertake equally well will inevitably erode Jewish identity and solidarity. If Jewishness means a certain position on aid to parochial schools, laws regulating abortion, support for the Legal Services Corporation, or gun control, nothing distinguishes it from secular life and there is no uniquely *Jewish* bond that can maintain the cohesion of the Jewish community.

The Holocaust

Commemorations of the Holocaust can, by contrast, provide a uniquely Jewish bond, and such ceremonies are playing an increasing role in Jewish public life. That role, however, may also be perverse. Attention to the Holocaust has reached a high point only now, a half-century after its end. In the 1950s and 1960s, when there were numerous signs of institutional vigor in the American Jewish community, it was synagogues that were being built—not museums commemorating the Holocaust. Survivors were rarely heard from in public, and American Jewish life was able to focus on Israel without too much thought about the events that had led to that state's founding. College courses on the Holocaust were extremely rare. When Nathan Glazer wrote his classic *American Judaism* in 1957, he did not even mention the Holocaust; as he later said, the emergence of the Holocaust in American Jewish consciousness was one of the great surprises of postwar Jewish life in America. Today literally hundreds of campuses allow students to study the Holocaust, and American Jews have learned far more about what happened to their coreligionists in Europe, and about the failings of their own government in dealing with the war against the Jews of Europe, than they had previously known. The demands of history are being met. In fact, 85 percent of American Jews say the Holocaust is very important to their sense of being Jewish. *Fewer Jews say that about God, the Torah, or any other factor.*[70]

No doubt the 1967 War had its impact. The reminder to American Jews that millions of other Jews were still in peril brought back memories of a past, then much closer, when such peril had existed and turned into mass murder. But it is difficult to escape the conclusion that the greatly increased place of the Holocaust in American Jewish consciousness is a phenomenon that should not be celebrated. It may not last—and perhaps it should not.

To begin with, the impact of the Nazis' war against European Jewry reflects at least in part the moral and psychological impact of the testimony of Holocaust survivors. As the years pass, there will be fewer and fewer of them to tell their stories and to bear witness, and the direct personal impact of their lives and their suffering will diminish. As it diminishes, the emotional impact of the Holocaust surely cannot be expected to sustain Jewish identity.

And even now the tremendously greater awareness of the Holocaust has seemed to have little effect on the actual behavior of American Jews. Certainly it cemented American Jewish support for Israel; for just as the 1967 War revived memories of the Holocaust, the Holocaust itself was the conclusive proof for most American Jews that creation and then defense of a Jewish state should be a central goal of their community. But as has been discussed, the power of that emotional link to Israel will decline as the risk to the Jewish state appears to decline. As the Holocaust itself and as Israel's wars recede into the past, their combined impact on the consciousness of American Jews cannot be counted on to sustain Jewish identity in America.

It is a fact that the Holocaust "revival" has not slowed the assimilationist trends American Jews are decrying; that is, study of the Holocaust has spread precisely during the years when intermarriage has as well, and ritual observance and synagogue affiliation have declined. If increased knowledge and feeling about the Holocaust are having an influence on the vigor of Jewish identity and solidarity, it is very hard to see. Survivors themselves aside, what, after all, is demanded of American Jews when they focus on that catastrophe? A one-time contribution to building a museum? A visit there to see the finished product? As Rabbi Jacob Neusner has said, this "Judaism of Holocaust and Redemption" allows American Jews "to be intensely Jewish, but only once in a while, providing a means of expressing difference in public and in politics while not exacting much of a cost in meaningful everyday difference from others."[71]

Unlike a real commitment to Judaism, commemorating the Holocaust is for many Jews quite convenient. This is not to denigrate the work of those who have made it their cause, much less to suggest that Holocaust survivors are taking an easy way out when they decide to record and communicate their experiences to us. But for most American Jews, remembering the Holocaust is neither a significant commitment of time nor a great and life-changing passion. Nor is it even, for most American Jews today, an exercise in memory, for the vast majority are too young to have any memory of those years. It is instead a form of melodrama, putting oneself in the shoes of those European Jews in the 1930s and 1940s. This permits a deeper understanding of the terrors those Jews felt and the horrors they suffered. But does it produce something positive? Rabbi Neusner does not think so. He writes that Judaism has always emphasized the moments when God saved the Jewish people (which are commemorated in the holidays of Passover, Purim, and Tabernacles), while the moments of destruction and tragedy became minor fast days. "In fact," he goes on,

> Judaic piety has all along known how to respond to disaster. For those for whom the classic Judaic symbolic structure remains intact, the Holocaust changes nothing. For those to whom classical Judaism offers no viable option, the Holocaust changes nothing.[72]

This was true even inside the death camps: most survivors who entered with a deep religious commitment emerged as observant Jews, while those who entered without faith left without it.

What, then, is the conclusion? It was drawn by the Orthodox scholar Michael Wyschograd in his article on "Faith and the Holocaust" a quarter century ago: "There is no salvation to be extracted from the Holocaust, no faltering Judaism can be revived by it, no new reason for the continuation of the Jewish people can be found in it."[73]

A Jewish community organized around Jewish victimization, suffering, tragedy, and death is unlikely to attract the passion of new generations. Focus on the Holocaust instead of on Judaism is more likely to inculcate hatred, fear, and resentment of Christians, and of Germans in particular (or to justify such feelings when they already exist) than to reinforce any positive Jewish identity, any profound Jewish faith, or any strict pattern of Jewish ritual observance. Putting the memory of the Holocaust at the center of Jewish identity is, moreover, a distortion of the true faith of Israel—faith in the election and redemption, not the abandonment, of the Jewish people by their God. The Holocaust is an immense tragedy that all Jews must study and come to terms with, as they must come to terms with the long history of Jewish suffering. But it is not the cement that will hold American Jews together.

Can Anti-Semitism Help?

In the eyes of many American Jews, anti-Semitism is still a very significant problem. A 1988 survey of American Jews conducted for the American Jewish Committee found that 57 percent felt they "could one day face severe anti-Semitic persecution." A large minority, 41 percent, felt that "Jews are widely disliked by Gentile Americans," and more than one-fourth agreed that "As a Jew, I don't feel totally safe in America."[74] When asked whether they agreed that "Anti-semitism is currently not a serious problem for American Jews," only 14 percent assented, while 76 percent disagreed with the proposition.[75]

What is more, fear of anti-Semitism "plays a vital role in the Jewish identity of contemporary American Jews."[76] Ellen Willis, a secular and left-wing Jew writing in the *Village Voice,* expressed this attitude plainly.

> It seems like such a negative thing to define Jewish identity in terms of anti-Semitism. But I've come to the conclusion that that's really a false issue, because the very identity of the Jews—who we are in history, what we represent—is totally bound up with anti-Semitism. . . . Every Jew is a victim of anti-Semitism—a member of a pariah people.[77]

To many American Jews like Ellen Willis, the fight against anti-Semitism is the very heart of being Jewish. And of course if anti-Semitism is central to "who we are in history," hostility toward Christians and Christianity will reflect not the actual level of anti-Semitism but its role in Jewish identity. For this reason, the historian Edward Shapiro wrote, it was "difficult for [secular Jews] not to exaggerate the extent of American anti-Semitism. Otherwise they would have had either to admit that the most important element in their own Jewish identity was no longer relevant or redefine their Jewish identity in more positive ways."[78] Thus a deep-seated fear of Christianity and an expectation of anti-Semitism remain central to the "Jewishness" of many American Jews. For them, Jewishness does not consist of belief in traditional Judaism; instead, at the core it means not being Christian. That negative identity is strengthened by fearful presumptions about Christian attitudes toward Jews and their place in American society.

The problem with anti-Semitism as a source of Jewish identity is that with a decrease of prejudice those shored-up ramparts will collapse—and this is precisely what is happening in the United States. Intermarriage rates alone demonstrate that barriers among the many ethnic and religious groups here have fallen. Anti-Semitism and its impact on the lives of American Jews are declining. Not so many years ago, anti-Semitism was likely to affect where young Jews went to college, got a job, bought a house—and found a spouse. Those days are over and they will not return.*

All the data show anti-Semitism declining, at least among

---

*In his first term in the White House President Clinton had two Supreme Court appointments to make, and both were Jews—yet this fact was little mentioned in the press and was obviously no deterrent to their selection or confirmation. Jews sit in record numbers in the U.S. Congress as well. But many American Jews are reluctant to acknowledge the good news, as this example shows: "according to a 1985 survey by the whites. In fact surveys show enormous drops in anti-Semitism from a time, in the 1930s, when half of all non-Jews "harbored strong negative feelings toward Jews."[79] Those feelings declined after World War II, no doubt in part owing to the association of anti-Semitism with Nazi Germany and the Holocaust. Several times in the postwar period, Jews feared that some event would give rise to a great increase in anti-Semitism, but none did: not the Rosenberg spy case, not the McCarthy era, and not the 1973 Arab oil embargo against the United States for support of Israel.

The post-World War II years saw the rise of the civil rights movement, a crusade for racial justice and against bigotry. Jews understood that America's forceful embrace of tolerance as a prime national objective would benefit them as well as American blacks, and they threw themselves into civil rights work. As a result of that movement, a bevy of local, state, and federal laws now exist, backed by a broad public consensus, prohibiting and punishing displays of prejudice and acts of discrimination. Bigotry and anti-Semitism are now deeply disreputable in America and survive at the political extremes represented by the radical right and the Muslim left. Meanwhile, educational levels have been rising steadily, and American prosperity has included larger and larger segments of the population. Americans thus have fewer of the old motivations—such as ignorance and envy—to fall into anti-Semitism, and have internalized the society's harsh critique of all forms of racial and religious prejudice.

Today, about 20 percent of the population hold some anti-Semitic beliefs, and those who may be described as hard-core anti-

San Francisco Jewish Community Relations Council, almost a third of the Jews in one northern California region said that they did not think non-Jews would vote for a Jew for Congress. At the time they said this, all three of their elected Representatives in that area were Jewish." Earl Raab, "High Anxiety," *Present Tense* 15 (January–February 1988): 46.

Semites are perhaps 5 percent of the population.[80] An exhaustive study of surveys of public attitudes toward Jews was conducted by the American Jewish Committee in 1994. It found that though anti-Semitism still exists, it continues to decline in the United States, and that "negative stereotypes about Jews have diminished."[81] As younger whites in the surveys were significantly more tolerant than their elders, one can predict that the decline in anti-Semitism among whites will continue. In his 1994 book on *Anti-Semitism in America,* Leonard Dinnerstein concluded:

> Today antisemitism in the United States is neither virulent nor growing. It is not a powerful social or political force. . . . Much less prejudice exists in our own time than in any other period in the history of this nation. . . . There is no reason to suspect that antisemitism will not continue to decline in the United States. . . . the obvious conclusion is that it has declined in potency and will continue to do so for the foreseeable future.[82]

Anti-Semitism appears to be growing among American blacks, and although there has been little careful study of the problem, surveys suggest that "black Americans remain considerably more likely than white Americans to hold anti-Semitic views."[83] "Leaders" such as Louis Farrakhan voice the most vicious anti-Semitic sentiments, and these words have not rendered Farrakhan and his colleagues untouchables for the black political establishment. This anti-Semitic message has received a sympathetic hearing from all too many black audiences—not least on college campuses, where tomorrow's black elites are being educated. "While Black anti-Semitism is not a major force at present," an ADL study concluded, "it is the only potential source of an invigorated anti-Semitism that is being pushed by leaders with nontrivial followings."[84]

What is the impact on American Jews? There is always the danger that the anti-Semitism of certain black groups such as Farrakhan's Nation of Islam will turn toward violence. While organized violence may seem far-fetched, incidents such as the Crown Heights, Brooklyn, assault on Jews in 1991 (discussed in the following chapter) show that violent talk can inspire violent actions. There is as well the fear that once the taboo on public expression of anti-Semitism is broken by blacks, whites harboring similar views will rush forward to express them. And in fact white anti-Semitism has been increasingly visible in recent years in words and actions of various "militias" (odd assortments of extremists who share racist and chauvinistic views and often organize paramilitary groups aimed at resisting what they imagine to be the encroachment of national and international authorities on their liberties). An ADL report noted "the presence in some of them—even in leadership roles—of persons with histories of racial and religious bigotry and of political extremism."[85]

The key question is how any of this will affect Jewish identity in America, and the answer must be that it appears unlikely to do so. With respect to blacks, even assaults on poor Hasidic Jews are unlikely to have much impact on the lives of most American Jews—and in fact have not. Black anti-Semitism is likely to make Jews angry at the blacks who express it, and perhaps rupture the historically close and cooperative ties between many black and Jewish organizations. But it does not make Jews feel under assault by or isolated from the mainstream of, nor does it reduce their ability to integrate into, American society.

The same is true of extremist white anti-Semitism. Jews do not seem to be the target of the militias: the American Jewish Committee reported in mid-1995 that although there is much anti-Semitism in the "philosophy" of the militias, "the targets of the more extreme militia groups are not exclusively, or even primarily, Jews or other minorities. Environmentalists are also vilified. But most despised are government officials."[86] The key point, though, is not whom the militias hate the most but whether other Americans share that hatred. The danger exists, as it does from all expression of anti-Semitism, that the militias'—like the Black Muslims'—use of crude anti-Semitic rhetoric will lower the barriers preventing such hate speech in American society at large and stir up anti-Semitic attitudes. It can also be argued that such anti-Semitic language reflects very high underlying levels of anti-Semitism. Yet so far, happily, neither seems to be true, and the hatred spewed out by such groups appears to isolate them and not Jews from the American mainstream.

The 1996 political efforts of Pat Buchanan—who as a newspaper columnist and television personality expressed ill-concealed anti-Semitic sentiments—made many Jews wonder once again about the breadth of anti-Semitism in the United States. But his campaign demonstrated that among whites at least anti-Semitism remains a commodity difficult to sell. Buchanan abandoned any sign of overt anti-Semitism during his campaign and defended himself from charges of bigotry by claiming that "we've got rabbis on the board of our campaign."[87] In other words, knowing that anti-Semitism would cost him votes rather than gain him votes, he fled from past anti-Jewish statements. The point is not that he was sincere in doing so, but rather that this hypocrisy was—as Dr. Johnson defined it—the tribute vice pays to virtue. And in American politics, anti-Semitism is a vice.

So while anti-Semitism can unquestionably play a perverse but powerful role in promoting Jewish solidarity, in America that role is bound to decline, for anti-Semitism has become the mark of extremism rather than a facet of polite society. Such anti-Semitism as exists is as disgusting as ever and perhaps more visible than it was a few years ago, but it has had little real impact on the lives of American Jews. As Irving Kristol once wrote, "The danger facing American Jews today is not that Christians want to persecute them but that Christians want to marry them."[88]

The End of "Ethnicity"

Recently a famous Wall Street figure now in his sixties, who had been raised in a traditional and observant Jewish home, complained to Richard Joel, the national director of Hillel, asking why his children were not "more Jewish." He was perplexed and unhappy at their lack of connection and commitment to Jewish life, especially after he and his wife had tried hard to convey their own sense of involvement. He wondered "what I had that they didn't." Joel responded quickly: "Your mother." This piece of Jewish humor is also a piece of Jewish sociology, and captures the passing of the immigrant generations *and their children.*

"Jewishness" as an ethnic trait was a powerful bond not only for Jewish immigrants but for their children as well. As recently as two generations ago the vast majority of American Jews spoke Yiddish; now, Yiddish speakers are elderly people, and they are not being replaced by new immigrants bringing a rich Jewish culture to America with them. For a century and a half Jewish life in America had been reinforced and reinvigorated by the arrival of people steeped in Jewish culture, education, ritual practice, and the Yiddish language. Today, the only large numbers of Jewish arrivals are from the former Soviet Union, and these immigrants tend to be even more ignorant about Judaism than their American hosts. Classic works of American Jewish language and humor such as Leo Rosten's *The Education of Hyman Kaplan* and *The Joys of Yiddish* would not, if written today, enjoy the appreciative audiences they received in the 1950s, 1960s, and 1970s. For the newest generations of American Jews, the immigrant experiences and Yiddish culture they describe are nearly as distant and unfamiliar as the French Revolution.

Ethnicity, which acted as the single most powerful agent of Jewish communal solidarity for a century in America, is now being

dissolved in the heat of the melting pot. "Ethnic tasks and memories," Rabbi Arthur Hertzberg wrote in 1989 in *The Jews In America,* "could not stop the erosion of Jewishness." But this was not
because America demanded assimilation into the old Yankee
Protestant culture; rather, it was because the melting pot was ca-
pacious and permitted Jews and everyone else to feel at home.
"American society no longer forces assimilation into a dominant
culture," Hertzberg added. "It is possible in this new age of America to evaporate out of being Jewish without making a decision to
be anything else."[89] A sense of Jewish ethnicity remains powerful
for many Jews, and it is a factor in the Jewish identity of most. It
can and does strengthen ties to the Jewish community, but alone—
absent a commitment as well to Judaism—it cannot sustain them.
This will be true for nearly all Jews in twenty-first-century America, but it is especially true for the increasing percentage of Jews
whose ethnic background is mixed because they are the children of
intermarriage.

With the immigration of people steeped in Yiddish culture at an
end, intermarriage at an all-time high, and the population dispers-
ing from dense urban centers into a more typical American pattern,
it is foolish to hope that ethnicity can maintain the size and vitality
of the American Jewish community.

Most of the American Jewish community has abandoned *Judaism
the religion.* The old *Judaic* commandments to keep the Sabbath
day, to worship, to observe the dietary laws have given way. But the
substitute faiths American Jews devised in an effort to stay Jewish
while achieving success in America are failing. Far from saving
American Judaism, they threaten its future.

For people born in immigrant communities or to immigrant
parents and saturated with Jewish culture, it was possible to feel
"Jewish" and stay "Jewish" even without any involvement with

Judaism. But it is now clear that it is not possible to transmit this irreligious "Jewishness" successfully, as the Hebrew prayers have it, *l'dor vador*—from one generation to the next. Such "Jewishness" is a counterfeit faith, a passing phenomenon that will outlast the immigrants by only a few generations. The demographic data already suggest this, and the sense of crisis within the community reflects the increasingly widespread conclusion that it is so. In the end, as always in Jewish history, substitutes for Judaism are false idols and following them is a path to ruin.

The exact opposite of what American Jews expected is now happening. Jewish life that is not centered on Judaism is already disappearing in America, while traditional Judaism—and above all, Orthodoxy—which was expected to disappear, is stubbornly holding on.

Chapter 7

THE ORTHODOX NUISANCE

ORTHODOX Judaism was confidently expected to die out in an increasingly secular America. Its predicted demise was not much mourned by American Jews. The Jewish strategy for success in America, with its requirement of "social invisibility" and its struggle for a secular society, could be thwarted by the actions and beliefs of Christians. But the strict ritual requirements of Judaism, and the Jews who clung to them, could also thwart the strategy and thus became a source of danger. Jews who did not agree to seek that "invisibility" or assimilation, and to redefine their Jewishness in ways that did not interfere with the process, became isolated from the Jewish mainstream (not least in the Supreme Court, as the cases reviewed in Chapter Two showed) and, far from receiving the community's praise for their orthodoxy, became targets of its scorn.

The Orthodox Stand Alone

The Orthodox have disproved the forecast that the disappearance of traditional Judaism was inevitable, by rejecting the community's approach to Judaism and Jewishness. As Charles Liebman has suggested, they have resolutely refused to join the Jewish mainstream. Orthodoxy had to withdraw from the larger Jewish community,

165

which was enthusiastically embracing modern culture in all its forms, because its goal was "to counteract the experience of modernity." The whole core of Orthodox faithfulness to traditional Jewish conduct requires "the withdrawal from and rejection of modernity."[1] Far from seeking to maximize their influence in Jewish community organizations, the Orthodox were often seeking only to prevent their own "contamination" by the secularism of those organizations. No doubt the view that association with non-Orthodox Jews might bring some form of contamination was understood and resented by those at whom it was directed. And more generally, even if the Orthodox can be forgiven for their critical attitude toward other forms of Judaism, they cannot be excused the contempt that has sometimes all too visibly accompanied it.

The end result has been a deepening rift, now decades old, between Orthodox and non-Orthodox Jews.* Jewish religious conduct is increasingly divided, with "a large population of Jews moving toward religious minimalism and a minority gravitating toward greater participation and deepened concern for religion."[2] Between the two groups there is little sympathy, and the division is exacerbated by class prejudice. Tom Dine, for years the director of the American Israel Public Affairs Committee (the Jewish community's main organization for lobbying in support of Israel), characterized the problem memorably:

> I don't think mainstream Jews feel very comfortable with the ultra-Orthodox. It's a class thing, I suppose. Their image is—smelly. . . . United Jewish Appeal people have told me several times they don't

---

*Dividing the community into Orthodox and non-Orthodox is a form of shorthand. A more accurate division for this discussion is between those who follow traditional rituals such as daily synagogue prayer, eating only kosher food, and respecting the Sabbath, and those who do not. A small percentage of Conservative Jews, and all Reform Jews, do not. Accordingly, the division between Orthodox and non-Orthodox is a useful proxy for observant and nonobservant, although it is not entirely accurate.

want to fly El Al because of "those people.". . . It's low-class, like the Orthodox. Yes, that's still the image. Still the poor immigrant image.[3]

The attitude that Dine describes, and more generally resentment of and distaste for Orthodox and other traditionally observant Jews, is extremely widespread. The refusal of an observant Jew to ride on the Sabbath or to eat nonkosher foods, for example, is rarely accorded respect and admiration by the nonobservant Jewish majority, and is more often regarded as a nuisance. The wearing of visible symbols of Judaic traditionalism, such as a skullcap, fringed garment, or long earlocks, seems to make many other Jews ill at ease or even to repel them, rather than to elicit their solidarity.

Such attitudes can directly affect community policy toward Jews who are out of step with mainstream goals and behavior patterns. A disturbing but emblematic episode, recently brought to light in Hillel Levine and Lawrence Harmon's *Death of an American Jewish Community,* occurred in the 1960s in Boston. The Jewish neighborhoods of Roxbury, Mattapan, and Dorchester had existed for decades, housing some ninety thousand Jews. But as the result of deliberate targeting by Boston's banks and its corporate and civic establishment, "more than fifty years of Jewish settlement were overturned during a two-year period from 1968 to 1970."[4] In essence, poor blacks were granted housing assistance to move into those Jewish neighborhoods, and only those neighborhoods; crime rates rose and they soon became unlivable for the mostly poor and elderly Jews who remained there, close to each other and to the synagogues where they had worshipped for decades.

The needs of those Jews were ignored by the Jewish community leadership, whose attitude was termed "wholesale indifference" by a rabbi in the area.[5] Despite the clamoring of the Jews still living in the increasingly dangerous old neighborhoods, the major Jewish organizations stood silent. Boston's mayor later remarked that "I'm not knocking here but I don't remember anybody from the United Jewish Appeal. The Jewish community was not making noise." Onto this stage walked members of the Jewish Defense League, the radical activist group founded by the late Meir Kahane, which scornfully characterized the community leadership's views: "The fallacy in their thinking lies in that they look for acceptance and love of the Jew by the gentile world by painting the portrait of the Jew as 'we are just like you—therefore, love us and take us into your country club.'"[6]

This was a telling point, and it proved impossible in the Boston case to mobilize Jewish community support for Jews who refused—by their religious practices, and by their insistence on staying in an old Jewish neighborhood rather than moving to the suburbs—to live in accordance with that fundamental strategy of integration and "social invisibility."

A more recent example came in the Hasidic neighborhood of Crown Heights, Brooklyn, in 1991. On August 19, a black child was accidentally struck and killed when a car from the entourage of the Lubavitcher sect's leader jumped the sidewalk. The Jewish newspaper *Forward* reported what happened in the aftermath:

> Rioting erupted, and a Chasidic student, Yankel Rosenbaum, was killed while walking in the neighborhood. Jews hid in their back rooms and basements, in a state of fear reminiscent of the pogroms of the Pale. Yet, with one or two exceptions, it took the Jewish leadership in New York and the New York-based leaders of national Jewish organizations days, even weeks in some cases, to grasp the significance of what was happening, and their leadership, or lack of it, is still being talked about more than three years later as having been in default.
>
> In the immediate hours and days of the riot, statements were too slow to be issued and too often portrayed African Americans and Cha-

sidim as equally victimized. It took until Aug. 31 for mainstream Jewish organizations to label the violence in Crown Heights anti-Semitic.[7]

Two years later the split between Jewish elites and the more religious and poorer Jews was characterized by the *Forward* as "the ever-widening gap between the Jews of Park Avenue and the Jews of Canarsie and Kew Gardens." Resentment at wealthier, more liberal, more secular Jews was, the newspaper reported, "increasingly shared in outer-borough Jewish communities, where some people are still bitter about the seemingly languorous way many Manhattan-based Jewish organizations reacted to the Crown Heights riot."[8]

But the refusal of mainline Jewish organizations to support Orthodox Jewry has not been limited to individual incidents, no matter how significant. The secret of Orthodoxy's survival—and latterly vigorous revival—has been its educational system. The Jewish establishment has consistently opposed public support for those schools—and until very recently withheld its own as well.

The Day School Fight

The heart of the Orthodox community is its private school system. Where once a full yeshiva education was reserved for the small percentage of the population preparing for the rabbinate, today a K-to-12 day school system includes the vast majority of Orthodox youth, and many from non-Orthodox homes, male and female. In fact full-time Jewish education in America today is largely Orthodox education: 500 of the 625 Jewish day schools in the United States are Orthodox.[9] Of all the children attending Jewish day schools, 68 percent attend Orthodox schools, while only 15 percent attend Conservative-run schools, 14.5 percent attend community-sponsored multidenominational schools, and just 2.5 percent attend day schools sponsored by the Reform movement.[10]

The commitment to a separate school system has marked off the Orthodox from the rest of the Jewish community. In fact as the mostly Orthodox day school enrollment has risen, attendance by mostly non-Orthodox children at afternoon or Sunday Hebrew school classes has dropped, a "reflect[ion of] the polarization that is occurring among American Jews between a religiously devoted minority and an increasingly secularized majority."[11]

This polarization has had a large impact, in part because most American Jewish organizations have staked out positions far more supportive—whatever their rhetoric—of the large portion of American Jews offering their children little or no Jewish education. Given the importance that religious schooling holds for the Orthodox, some ability to get access to the taxes they pay to support the public schools they do not use is vital. But the major American Jewish organizations have been unremittingly hostile to this desire, as their briefs—and their alliances—in the important Supreme Court cases demonstrated. The bitter division between Orthodox and non-Orthodox Jewish groups was clear in 1993 in California, where a ballot proposition would have provided every student with a tuition voucher that could be used at secular or religious schools. Backing the initiative (known as "Proposition 174") were the Union of Orthodox Jewish Congregations, Agudath Israel of California, the Rabbinical Council of California, and Chabad-Lubavitch. Opposing it was virtually every non-Orthodox Jewish organization, including the Jewish Federation Council of Greater Los Angeles, B'nai B'rith, Hadassah, the [Reform] Union of American Hebrew Congregations, the American Jewish Congress, and the American Jewish Committee.[12]

The fight about day schools and school finances is central, not marginal, to the future of American Jewry, for religious education is invaluable in transmitting Judaism from one generation to the next. "Jewish education," the National Jewish Population Study revealed, "is one of the most effective tools for producing Jewishly identified adults [and] more extensive forms of Jewish education are closely associated with greater Jewish identification."[13] Not surprisingly, Jewish education seems to reduce intermarriage as well. Sylvia Fishman and Alice Goldstein of Brandeis report that the impact of extensive Jewish education

> is demonstrated in almost every area of public and private Jewish life. . . . extensive Jewish education is related to a greater ritual observance, greater likelihood of belonging to and attending synagogues, greater levels of voluntarism for Jewish causes, and greater chances of marrying a Jew and being opposed to intermarriage among one's children.[14]

An analysis of the 1990 National Jewish Population Study performed for the Avi Chai Foundation similarly concluded that "Jewish day schools are the best vehicles" for raising the level of involvement in Jewish religious and communal activities. "The data show a strong correlation between Jewish education and intermarriage rates. . . . Similarly, attitudes toward intermarriage are also strongly affected by Jewish education." The study noted that "the great majority of day schoolers are married within the faith (79%), versus less than half of those who studied in other types of Jewish schools." As to charitable endeavors, "54% of those who have had Jewish education contributed, while only 28% of those who have had no Jewish education gave something. In addition, there is a direct correlation: the more years of Jewish education, the more the individual gives." Three percent of Sunday school graduates gave over $1,000 per year to Jewish causes, which 17 percent of day school graduates did.[15]

If the Jewish community is serious about its continuity and survival, support for day schools is an essential step. Not because most American Jewish children will attend them, even if tuitions are low. Today, despite reasonably low tuitions, only about one-fourth of all Catholic elementary school age children attend Catholic schools, and the figure is less than 20 percent for high school age children.[16] The vast majority of Jewish day schools in the United States are Orthodox yeshivas, and it is nearly impossible to conceive of circumstances in which majorities of non-Orthodox children would attend day school.[17] But with better funding and more community support, more would do so than do today. This would strengthen the American Jewish community, because day school graduates will be well-educated Jews and—as the data show quite conclusively—are far more likely to be observant Jews, marry Jews, and raise their children as Jews.

But American Jewry has been remarkably unsupportive of religious education. One need only compare the attitude of the Catholic Church toward its own day schools to see the difference. Catholic schools educate about 2.6 million students, half of all the private school students in the country, in 8,731 parochial schools—and enrollment is growing steadily. Catholics spend over $5 billion a year supporting these elementary and secondary schools. Across the nation, Catholic schools receive the assistance of a network of over 122,000 unpaid volunteers.[18]

There is no real equivalent among Jews, and the *Forward* reported in 1995 that "private Jewish day schools are considerably more expensive than their Catholic counterparts." Moreover, "few sources of financial aid are being made available to Jewish families who long to give their children Jewish educations but can't afford the steep prices." Scholarship funds exist but are "hard to obtain, and the process of application is daunting and humiliating." The director of one Jewish day school told the *Forward* that enrollment could be doubled if tuitions could be brought down. The more expensive Jewish day schools, such as New York's Ramaz school, charge a high school tuition of $12,500 per year, an amount simply unheard of among Catholic day schools (where typically high school tuition is about $3,000).[19] Such scholarships as are available often focus on new immigrants, and rich families can pay the tuitions, leaving the middle class high and dry. Thus a family earning $50,000 or $75,000 per year, having three children, and trying to save for their college education cannot possibly afford ten, twenty, or thirty thousand dollars for secondary school education.

Until now, the American Jewish community has funded day schools poorly itself and strongly opposed any form of tax relief or tuition vouchers that would help the Jewish parents trying to pay for them. The vehement opposition of the Jewish establishment and Jewish liberals to school vouchers that would, in the main, go for religious-sponsored schools is especially notable because it trumped arguments that might otherwise have appealed to their liberalism. After all, the Catholic schools that would receive the bulk of such vouchers are the only alternative for many ghetto parents seeking to keep their children out of disastrous public schools. Often, the school population in inner-city Catholic schools is substantially non-Catholic, including many nonwhite Protestant students seeking a better education. In fact, 23 percent of all students in Catholic schools are nonwhite, and 12 percent are non-Catholic.[20] A remarkable two-thirds of black students in Catholic schools are non-Catholic.[21]

The most striking discussion of the issue of public support for religious and private education came in a 1994 presentation at Princeton University by Diane Ravitch, a former assistant secretary of education and—until then—a staunch critic of tuition tax credits, vouchers, and other plans to provide financial relief for parents with students in nonpublic schools. First, Ravitch explained that it was no answer to say "improve the public schools," for decades have passed without that incantation's having the slightest impact; the public schools seem to get worse. That is why so many families want to escape them. "It is not just," she said,

> to compel poor children to attend bad schools. It is not just to prohibit poor families from sending their children to the school of their choice, even if that school has a religious affiliation. It is not just to deny free schooling to parents with strong religious convictions, any more than it would be just to prohibit the use of federal scholarships in non-public universities (like Notre Dame, Marymount, Yeshiva, or even Princeton).[22]

Ravitch then wondered what we mean by "public school," anyway: "Thus, the paradox: a school in an exclusive suburb that educates affluent students at a cost of $15,000 per student per year is 'public,' while an inner city parochial school that educates impoverished minority students at a cost of $2,000 per year is not 'public.'"

Wealthy families can choose private school, or move to the suburbs, but the inner-city poor have no choice—unless something like a voucher system gives it to them. That solution would allow observant Jewish parents some relief as they seek a Jewish day school education, and could be of real assistance to the poorest parents as they, too, try to give their children the kind of start in life they most value.

Such an argument would seem likely to appeal to American Jews not only as Jews but as political liberals, but the Orthodox parents find that it is rejected out of hand. In 1995 a leading Conservative rabbi argued against vouchers on the grounds that "only in destitute, inner-city neighborhoods will public vouchers for the proposed $500 per child enable poor children to opt for low-cost private education. Certainly in the suburbs, several hundred dollars is not the breaking point between attending or avoiding prestigious prep schools."[23] Here a Jewish religious leader argues against vouchers despite their admitted usefulness for the poorest children, on the grounds that they do little good for the suburban rich!

No accommodation is permitted; in the view of most Jewish groups, the wall of separation must be an iron curtain. Nor can this position be defended by a simple reference to the Constitution, as if current interpretations of that document by the Supreme Court were cast in iron and not subject to challenge or change. In fact, most American Jews are very likely unaware of the bizarre state of the law regarding support for parochial schools. As Robert Bork has succinctly described it,

> Where religion is concerned . . . a state may lend parochial school-children geography textbooks that contain maps of the United States but may not lend them maps of the United States for use in a geography class; a state may lend parochial schoolchildren textbooks on American colonial history but not a film about George Washington; a state may pay for diagnostic services conducted in a parochial school but therapeutic services must be provided in a different building.[24]

Jewish opposition to aid for religious schools cannot, then, be defended as "mere" constitutionalism. There is a great argument over what the Constitution says on this matter, the current state of the law is extremely convoluted, and Jewish attitudes reflect powerful policy preferences rather than conclusions ineluctably drawn from the First Amendment. "Organizations like the American Jewish Committee might have found numerous reasons to modify their strict separationist stand," Naomi Cohen wrote in her 1972 history of the committee. Not only would it improve relations with the Orthodox but it would also smooth interreligious activities with

Christian groups that are made more difficult by strict separationism.* "Yet these considerations did not significantly alter the
Committee's position, which reflected an emotional and ideological
commitment more compelling than pragmatic reasoning," she
wrote in a conclusion still valid today.[25]

The Liberal Faith

When Orthodox views have conflicted with the liberal faith of most
American Jews—whether on church-and-state matters, education,
or "social" issues such as homosexuality and abortion—that liberal
faith has been completely dominant in the major non-Orthodox
American Jewish organizations. Neither the success of Orthodoxy
in America nor the demographic crisis of nonobservant Jewry has
led to much visible questioning of their public policy positions; in
the case of the American Jewish Committee, there has been debate
but no policy change.

Absent its deep—one might say "religious"—commitment to
secularism and its view that religion was a source of danger to Jews
in America, the rest of the Jewish community might have been
expected to react to traditionally observant Jews with admiration
and support. The requirements of Orthodoxy are many, and it is
far easier, in our culture, *not* to respect the Sabbath, *not* to attend
synagogue, *not* to keep a kosher home, *not* to wear the *kippah*

---

*The committee has in more recent years supported a great deal of invaluable scholar-
ship in the matter of Jewish continuity and has undertaken public advertising campaigns that place Judaism at its heart. In comparison with organizations such as the
American Jewish Congress, the committee's attitude toward Judaism per se is far more
welcoming, and there is, indeed, passionate debate within the committee's staff and lay
leadership over the balance between its traditional secularism and a new appreciation of
the role of religion. Still, in its positions on public policy issues the committee remains
wedded—as its amicus curiae briefs to the Supreme Court show—to the ideology it
championed in the past.

(skullcap); and resistance requires strong will and deep faith. Traditional Judaism is not an easy path to follow under any circumstances. Moreover, the Orthodox are doing something that should in principle attract the admiration and support of the American Jewish community: staying Jewish. They do not have a 52 percent intermarriage rate, and they are not suffering from a population decline. Far from disappearing or weakening, "this is the first generation in over 200 years . . . in which Orthodoxy is not in decline."[26]

Yet, instead of respect and encouragement for more traditional Jews, the Jewish community's attitude is often one of outright hostility. This remarkable lack of sympathy and respect for more observant Jews by less observant ones is one of the most striking aspects of American Jewish life today. There is a powerful resistance to the idea that faithfulness to traditional Judaism is in any way preferable to following the community's new, secular substitutes, or preferable to less demanding denominations within Judaism. Modern Jewish individualism allows each Jew to pick and choose, cafeteria style, within the Jewish tradition; as Leonard Fein put it, "I take what I need from the tradition, and what I like, and what I can, the parts that make substantive sense and the parts that have stylistic appeal."[27] The conclusion that this is inadequate and that Jewish law demands more—that God demands more—would be profoundly troubling to most American Jews. In fact, most would be more upset to learn that a child of theirs was to marry an Orthodox Jew and *become Orthodox* than that their child was marrying a non-Jew and was going to lead a secular existence.

One study found that only 18 percent of American Jews were willing to acknowledge that "Orthodox Jews are the most authentic Jews around," while 74 percent disagreed or disagreed strongly. The Orthodox assertion that faithfulness to Jewish law (*Halachah*) defines a good Jew is rejected, as are those who express it: when asked if they felt insulted by Orthodox Jews "who show no respect for the way you choose to be Jewish," 84 percent of American Jews said they were somewhat or very offended.[28]

No doubt this 84 percent includes many Jewish community leaders, who are accustomed to being treated in their own social circles as excellent, dedicated Jews devoting a tremendous amount of time to "Jewish" issues. Disrespect from the Orthodox must be particularly galling for them, and to be dismissed as bad Jews is too much for them to take—even if they are in fact nonobservant in every conceivable way. From the Orthodox perspective, the liberal activist and the Federation officer may be good citizens and good souls, but without any ritual observance they cannot be good *Jews*. The good Jew is ritually observant and resists assimilation, in some sense living apart, never fitting comfortably into American or any other society.

Worse yet, if traditional Judaism can thrive in America and other forms of "Jewishness" are dead ends, the Jewish community's excuses for abandoning the demands of the old faith are demolished. In fact the Orthodox and other observant and traditional Jews are a living rejection of the views and strategy, the excuses and weaknesses, of the American Jewish community. For if they can thrive in America and practice Judaism, why can't the rest of American Jewry do this as well? And if the community can but won't, doesn't it merit the contempt in which it believes the traditionally observant hold it? These are fearful and indeed abhorrent ideas for the American Jewish community, which has sought above all to be *comfortable* in America.

The Orthodox reject that goal, welcoming the separation and discomfort of being an observant Jew in a Christian society. They are saboteurs of the strategy of "social invisibility," and, worse yet, allies of the Christian groups that seek to increase religious influences in American society. Thus the Orthodox not only wound the pride of non-Orthodox Jewish leaders, but give aid and comfort to what most Jews view as political enemies whose doctrines may bring real danger to Jews.

The most divisive factor in American Jewish life is, then, Judaism. As the Chief Rabbi of England, Jonathan Sacks, phrased it, "Once the presence of God was believed to make peace between Jews. Now peace is believed to require his absence."[29] This judgment reflects the many battles among Orthodox, Conservative, and Reform Jews, and their widely divergent convictions on where Jewish interests lie. But it is now very clear that the "presence of God" is the only guarantee of Jewish continuity in America.

The focus of the American Jewish community must shift from how American Jews are doing, to how American Judaism is faring. A decision to place Judaism back in the center of Jewish life would mean that the American Jewish community must reevaluate its struggle for secularism. It would mean a rethinking of relations between Orthodox and non-Orthodox Jews. And it would require each Jew to rethink his own religious life and practices.

Chapter 8

RETURN

What do American Jews fear most, and want most?

THE ANSWER provided by their religion is that Jews must fear, above all else, God's righteous wrath, and seek above all to love God, keep His commandments, and teach them to their children. Outside the land of Israel, there can be no doubt that Jews, faithful to the covenant between God and Abraham, are to stand apart from the nation in which they live. It is the very nature of being Jewish to be apart—except in Israel—from the rest of the population. Will Herberg maintained that "in the last analysis, the Jew cannot really be totally adjusted to his environment. . . . He is the very embodiment of non-adjustment. He cannot so identify himself with any culture, society, or institution that he no longer lives in tension with it."[1] The separation is metaphysical and implies life in neither a psychological nor a physical ghetto nor, as anti-Semites would have it, any disloyalty to the land in which the Jew lives. It implies, rather, a state of mind in which Jews acknowledge their participation in a covenant now five thousand years old and extending endlessly into the future.

Instead, American Jews fled from this traditional belief, fearing precisely the "apartness" that Judaism demands. For a century, they have acted as if they were threatened by religion—by both the religion of most of their fellow citizens and the unique requirements of their own. A society in which the distinctions between Jew and Christian were strong seemed to them dangerous. As the late Lucy Dawidowicz said, American Jews see religion not through the filter of the American Revolution but of the French: progress requires "the elimination of religion from society."[2] And most Jews have long believed that there is no risk, either for the society as a whole or for them as Jews, from that diminished role for religion. In this, of course, they have been wrong.

Are the Orthodox Right?

The decline of the American Jewish community has created fears and pressures, but the changes that would be required to stop that decline give rise to equally potent fears and pressures. It is difficult enough to rethink the public policy prescriptions that have for so long had almost automatic Jewish support. For most Jews the prospect of radical change in their own lives or in American Jewish life as a whole arouses greater anxiety than the prospect of further community decline.

For if the central issue of the day is, as virtually every major Jewish organization now says, "continuity," how can more deference to those most successful at "continuity" be avoided? If the key challenge is keeping one's children and grandchildren Jewish, do not the Orthodox and other traditionally observant Jews have the right to claim success—and to insist that their approach must be right? Obviously, this principle if too widely applied would eliminate Reform and Conservative Judaism entirely. The (Orthodox) Chief Rabbi of England, Jonathan Sacks, has argued that "Only Orthodox Judaism will enable the Jewish people to survive." He believes that "Orthodox Judaism bears . . . . the responsibility to lead the entire Jewish people. There is no alternative route to Jewish survival."[3]

But acknowledging Orthodox success does not imply that all American Jews, if they are serious about the survival of their community, must instantly become Orthodox. That would not be a serious proposal, for Orthodoxy requires a level of faith that most Jews simply do not have. Moreover, the term "Orthodoxy" covers a multitude of very varied forms of traditional Judaism, which range from modern Orthodox to truly separatist Hasidic sects. The world of Orthodoxy is divided among groups that seem to agree on only one thing: non-Orthodox Judaism is inauthentic.

But an open-minded look at Orthodoxy does mean that those Jews who are struggling unsuccessfully to keep their communities faithful to Judaism should listen carefully to those who are succeeding, and try to understand the secrets of that success.

They are succeeding not only by virtue of their acts—their adherence to ritual and their educational network—but also because of their conception of the Jew's place in our open society. They have created what is in essence a "counterculture," and they are seriously resistant to the prevailing trends in American social life. From teenage sex to abortion to homosexuality, and above all including secularism itself, they are at odds with the prevailing culture in which most Americans, and most American Jews, live.

Most American Jews will not join that counterculture, becoming fully observant religiously and sending their children to Jewish day schools (though a number are doing so, for educational rather than religious reasons). But what the American Jewish community must, as a collectivity, now do is to *offer respect, admiration, and support* to those Jews who do make that choice. Most who have made it are Orthodox, but it is worth repeating again that many are not. There are, for example, twenty thousand students in seventy-five

Conservative day schools, and thousands more non-Orthodox students in interdenominational community-run schools.

More broadly, the community must shift energy from its efforts to promote a secular society and to ensure that individual Jews can succeed in America, and focus instead on the goal of sustaining *Judaism* here. Return—*t'shuvah*—can be the collective decision of the community despite the unwillingness of many Jews to participate themselves.

Some elements of the Jewish community will not accept religion as the true basis and cement of the community's existence; for many Jewish activists a return to Judaism will never occur. Their loyalties are, by now, to secular causes disguised in Jewish trappings, and the religious content cannot be revived. They, along with the many Jews whose fears cannot be overcome, will resist tooth and nail the abandonment of American Jewry's secularist design.

A return to Judaism must, inevitably, leave some Jews by the wayside. Those who will have lost all religious faith are tied to the community only by brittle bonds of ethnic memory, family history, or personal interpretations of Judaism as a social and political force. They are free to entertain their own definitions of Judaism, but the organized Jewish community has no such luxury in the face of demographic disaster. Those who cannot be brought back to Judaism through "inreach," or indeed "outreach," may be lost to the community when it refocuses its efforts and resources. But the alternative, catering to marginal or to irreligious Jews, endangers the community as a whole.

For what is required in American Jewry now is a change in the publicly acknowledged goals and standards of the community. It would be a far cry from the present attitude of disdain, or at best indifference, that is so often directed at those Jews who reject the community's assimilationist norms. It would make the financing of religious education a central community activity, so that no Jewish family that seeks a religious education for its children is prevented by the issue of costs. It would mean making the link to Israel far less a matter of financial support, and far more one of personal contact and commitment.* It would mean bridging the gap between the lay organizations—above all, the Federations—and the community's religious institutions—its day schools and its synagogues.

Some of these programmatic changes have already begun, and in some communities they are far advanced. Moreover, the 1995 Report of the North American Commission on Jewish Identity and Continuity, a broad-based group convened by the Council of Jewish Federations, urges Jewish communities to move in this direction. The report concluded that Jewish continuity depends centrally on the work of synagogues and called upon federations to "take specific steps to promote synagogue membership and participation"; noted that "intensive Jewish education is our most powerful vehicle for . . . Jewish growth," and spoke of the "need to make day school education available and affordable to all who might want it."

But far more important than the necessary changes in budget or programs is the change in understanding. The new understanding would not be that Orthodoxy is better than the Conservative or Reform movements, but rather that the fundamental proposition on which the Orthodox operate is in fact correct: Judaism, not Jewish-

---

*The then deputy foreign minister of Israel, Yossi Beilin, stirred up a storm in 1994 when he told American Jews, "We do not need your money. We do not need charity anymore. Your own communities need it more than we do. They have their own problems and should use the money they raise internally." ("Bad Boy Beilin Seeks to Scrap Jewish Agency," *Forward,* July 1, 1994, p. 1.) Beilin proposed, among other things, a program that pays for a trip to Israel for every American Jewish teenager as one sensible alternative to today's communal activities. In fact, Jewish communities throughout the country are adopting versions of this program, using existing funding or raising special monies for this purpose. The idea of a trip to Israel as a universal rite of passage has spread fast—although the American Jewish community has very far to go before it is translated into a reality and adequate funding is made available.

ness, must be the heart of a Jew's life and of the community's life. While the recommendations of the Report of the North American Commission seem to point this way, the report—perhaps in an effort to gain and keep a consensus among its backers—does not quite say so. But the American Jewish community must conceive of itself as a *religious* community, or it will continue on its path to decline. There is only one real "continuity agenda" for American Jews. Every other effort to transmit Jewishness across the generations has failed. Only Judaism, as a religion, can perform this task. It follows, therefore, that the American Jewish community must reorganize its institutional life to acknowledge that fact.

Religion and American Life

In seeking a secular society, American Jews have been motivated not only by their conception of what was "good for the Jews"; they have also believed that a less religious America would be better for all Americans, for it would be more tolerant and more open-minded. But now they must confront American social problems and ask whether the decline of religion's role has made a contribution.

As the Jewish author and social critic Dennis Prager says, "I welcome a secular government in America, not a godless one, and I fear a secular and godless population. This Jew fears a post-Christian America. I had a glimpse of it during the riots in Los Angeles."[4] Robert Woodson, head of the black self-help organization called the National Center for Neighborhood Enterprise, tells this story: You are walking back to your car through a deserted downtown parking lot and a group of young black men start to enter the lot coming toward you. Do you feel any better, any safer, if you notice that each one is carrying a Bible and they seem to be either coming from or going to church?

That small story makes a large point, and it is one hardly limited to the religious or political right. In a 1995 speech on religion in America, President Clinton said

> this country needs to be a place where religion grows and flourishes. Don't you believe that if every kid in every difficult neighborhood in America were in a religious institution on the weekends . . . don't you really believe that the drug rate, the crime rate, the violence rate, the sense of self-destruction would go way down and the quality of the character of this country would go way up?[5]

In fact the last few decades have seen both the marginalization of the role of religion and its teachings about virtue, and an extraordinary decline in American morality. The late social critic Christopher Lasch described the "wholesale defection from standards of personal conduct—civility, industry, self-restraint—that were once considered indispensable to democracy."[6] The illegitimacy rate in the United States rose from 5 percent in 1960, to 11 percent in 1970, to 18 percent in 1980, and to 30 percent by 1991—a sixfold increase in thirty years. In 1970, 5 percent of fifteen-year-old girls had had sexual intercourse; by 1988, 25 percent had. The crime rate in the United States tripled between 1960 and 1980; and violent crime nearly quintupled between 1960 and 1990.[7] Is it really coincidental that these developments occurred not during the decades of Depression, unemployment, widespread poverty, and war but during those in which religion came to play a smaller and smaller role in American life?

Conversely, a large body of sociological data links religious practice and belief both to levels of self-declared personal happiness and to positive social phenomena such as lower rates of divorce, illegitimacy, teenage drug use, and even criminal activity.[8] What is more, individuals who attend church every week give more than three times as much to charity (as a percentage of their income) as those who never go to church, and are nearly twice as likely to be volunteers of some sort. These conclusions should hardly be surprising. The insight is the simple one that has been common among Americans since the Republic was founded. Republican institutions and a free economy do not create virtuous citizens, religion does. This was certainly the belief of George Washington, who in his Farewell Address described the central role religion might play in the new republic.

> Of all the dispositions and habits which lead to political prosperity, religion and morality are the indispensable supports. . . . And let us with caution indulge the supposition that morality can be maintained without religion. . . . reason and experience both forbid us to expect that national morality can prevail in exclusion of religious principle.

Washington and his contemporaries believed that religion was beneficial for the society regardless of the ultimate truth of the religion in question—or of any religion. American institutions were created to allow religion to fill that role yet not extend so far that it could limit the freedom of conscience of any citizen.

In this century we have seen two gigantic experiments at postreligious societies where the traditional restraints of religion and morality were entirely removed: Communism and Nazism. In both cases Jews became the special targets, but there was evil enough even without the scourge of anti-Semitism. For when the transcendental inhibition against evil is removed, when society becomes so purely secular that the restraints imposed by God on man are truly eradicated, minorities are but the earliest victims. "Inhuman" behavior turns out to be all too human unless the nations remember the commandments of their Creator.

No such wholesale abandonment of religion is likely in this, the most religiously observant country in the Western world. Yet with the decline of traditional morality here, American Jews have shared with their fellow citizens of all religions the effects of the "wholesale defection from standards of personal conduct" that Christopher Lasch described. Americans have seen in a small way what others have learned through much more painful lessons: in the wholly secular society, freedom often turns to license unbounded by moral limits.

Judaism in America

American Jews do not live in isolation from the rest of American society, and the influence of broader social and religious trends on American Jewish religious life is undeniable. Steven Cohen summed up the phenomenon in his book *American Modernity and Jewish Identity*:

> In an environment where religious behavior in the larger society is declining, there is good reason to anticipate parallel declines among Jews as well. Conversely, where and when religious interest and practice increase, similar changes may be expected among Jews, too.[9]

And in fact, as religion has been driven to the margins of American life, Jews have become less Jewish. This has come as a shock to most American Jews, but the late Seymour Siegel, a professor at the Jewish Theological Seminary, understood nearly thirty-five years ago where the Jewish community was taking itself—and how, and why. In 1963, Siegel called the idea that a "secular" culture is better for the Jewish community than a "religious" one "the first fallacy." In the past this had often been true, he said, given the levels of anti-Semitism that prevailed, and given that many Christian princes used their official power to harm and try to convert Jews. But this is America, and a very different danger confronts us. If we confine religious life to the church and the synagogue, the result will be a kind of "bland deism" that is the very antithesis of religious commitment—but is very likely to erode the Jewish community.[10]

Siegel knew what the rejoinder would be: that such a position would make it harder for American Jews to achieve the integration into American society that they seek. Jews and gentiles will feel more separated; Jewish schoolchildren will feel different from their classmates. Here is his striking reply:

> These contentions may or may not be true. However, this is the normative situation in *galut*. Jew *is* separated from gentile.

We should not even try to create a public life where differences between Jews and non-Jews are obliterated. If we succeed in eliminating religion from our culture, he said, driving religion from the public square,

> we will be in danger of creating a kind of bland, common Americanism which in the end will progressively wear away Jewish consciousness and commitment. The first ones to be converted to this idea of a post-Jewish, post-gentile culture will be the Jews. We will be digging our own graves—and ironically enough cheering on the gravediggers and spending money and effort to insure that no one takes away their shovels."[11]

Siegel's prediction is coming true: Jewish life is characterized by extremely low levels of religious observance and an intermarriage rate that will, left unchecked, diminish the community by half in the next two generations. Yet the American Jewish community has not abandoned the positions that have contributed to this result. Why not? In part because it fears another set of potential gravediggers, to borrow Siegel's term: American Christians. Still it clings to what is at bottom a dark vision of America, as a land permeated with anti-Semitism and always on the verge of anti-Semitic outbursts.

Jews did not think they needed to convert to Christianity to avoid these dangers; instead, America would convert, from a Christian society to one without religion. As Norman Podhoretz wrote, "Saint Paul, who was a Jew, conceived of salvation in a world in which there would be neither Jew nor Greek, and though he may have been the first, he was very far from the last Jew to dream of such a transcendence—transcendence of the actual alternative categories with which reality so stingily presents us. Not to be Jewish, but not to be Christian either."[12] That is what the American Jewish community aimed for, at least with regard to public life: to escape anti-Semitism by helping to create a nation where religion played a less and less important role. To avoid distinction from other citizens by diminishing the one factor that separated them from the overwhelming Christian majority.

There are, of course, societies in which the Jew is asked, do you mean to be one of us, or a Jew? There are still countries in which a non-Christian is forever an outsider, and Jews will forever be tolerated, marginal figures at best. The greatness of America lies in the fact that here it is not so. Here it is possible—even if it did not seem so to Jewish immigrants a century ago—to be a Jew and in every sense an American. Here Jews need not place their hopes for equality and opportunity in assimilation and in secularism. The tragedy is that American Jews are blind to this. The American Jewish community has not lived and embodied the American Dream; on the contrary, it has refused the opportunity America provided to remain fully Jews while they became fully Americans.

It is time to seize that opportunity and to put aside the fears of religion in America that led Jews down the secularist path. At some baseball stadiums today, there are kosher food stands, and one can see families of observant Jews lining up to buy kosher hot dogs before they take their seats. And in the capital dozens of Jews sit in Congress, some (like Senator Lieberman of Connecticut) sent there by the votes of Christian fellow citizens who were perfectly untroubled to elect an observant Jew. It will never be, and is not supposed to be, easy to be an observant Jew in America or anywhere else, but the calculation that a religious America endangers Jews is false and should be abandoned.

Can Jews insist that the country accommodate the needs of a religious minority? American Jews doubt that the society will respond favorably if such a small minority as they makes this demand. But this very demand is in fact being made today by devout Christians, who call upon American society and American law to accommodate the expression of religious faith.

The struggle over religion in America is rich with irony. The single group most damaged by the marginalization of religion is its most ardent defender, the Jews. This key religious minority has either abandoned the battlements when struggles over religion's role in society are being fought—or more often has switched sides. And the group most ardently decrying the marginalization of religion, evangelical Christians, has done little to reassure Jews of its break with past anti-Semitism. These two groups are far apart, yet have an extraordinary common interest: a society in which communities can thrive despite religious differences and notwithstanding their deviation from the religious or cultural mainstream.

Jews as individuals may prosper in an increasingly secular America, but no religious community can—not even the religion of the great majority of Americans, Christianity. This creates an opportunity for the devout in both religions, Christian and Jewish, to seize. To Jews, it is a chance to reach out to sectors of America where, in the past, anti-Semitism was deep. The American Jewish community's future is best guaranteed not in a secular society but in one that protects religious pluralism. And in that campaign for religious pluralism, it is long past time to recognize that in America, religious Christians are American Jewry's natural allies rather than natural enemies.

The fabulous successes of American Jews as individuals have coincided with their community's decline. American Jewry is beginning to evaporate before our eyes. Slowing that process will take a great effort and may meet with only partial success. The effort will, however, marshall the talents of American Jews and deepen their faith—as Jews and as Americans. It will strengthen them as a religious community and help build a society more welcoming to religious commitments. It will help bridge the gap between Christian and Jew. And above all, it will lay the foundation for building an American Jewish community grounded in faith and recommitted to the covenant of Sinai.

Faith

Whether American Jews can commit themselves anew to the goal of survival, to reversing the demographic patterns that threaten their collective future, depends on whether they still *believe they are above all else members of a religious community.* As an ethnic, cultural, or political entity they are doomed. Such identification erodes from one generation to the next; it cannot be sustained against the pressures of a society seeking relentlessly to include them within larger groups of citizens who do not share their religious heritage.

For the large non-Orthodox and nonpracticing majority, what does this mean? Whatever the Jewish community's institutions must do, what must they do as individuals? They must recognize, first, that Jewish ethnicity is no proof against American culture, and that American Jewry will survive as a religious community or not at all.

American Jews persuaded themselves that less was more: that less ritual observance, less synagogue attendance was somehow better for American Judaism. The vast majority of American Jews came to believe that traditional Judaism could not survive in America, and indeed should not; and this allowed them not only to stop practicing Judaism but to congratulate or at least defend themselves for doing so. As a result, we find not only remarkably low levels of observance among American Jews but even more remarkably high levels of self-satisfaction. Once it is understood that only Judaism can be transmitted reliably from generation to generation and that the flight from Judaism has proved disastrous, the conclusion is inescapable: the individual Jew must—as a member of a religious community—do more, and understand that more is indeed better.

The meaning of that "more" will vary for each individual, for each starts at a different level of observance. Judaism in any event presents a series of rules and tasks meant to control every waking moment. Jews are not enjoined to seek sainthood, but a reasonable goal is progress: to be a better Jew. For some individuals, this might mean learning Hebrew so as to understand the synagogue service; for others, studying the Torah; for still others, attendance at synagogue or removing nonkosher foods from their diet. No one can answer for another Jew the questions, how far and how fast must I go down this path? What can be asserted, however, is that the Jew who believes in the survival of the American Jewish community must be on the path.

And what of faith? Is it not a prerequisite for such religious activity? At first glance it does not appear to be so, for Jews can turn to Judaism as a means of Jewish survival. Judaism can be for them if not a faith then an instrumentality for achieving the social goal of perpetuating the group. Can Jewish nonbelievers troop off to synagogue, or light Sabbath candles, not because these are considered divine commands but because they make it more likely that the next generation will perform the same empty rituals? Cynics might suggest that this describes the behavior of many American Jews already, attending synagogue once a year at the High Holidays in a bow to tradition that reflects familial and social obligations rather than obedience to religious law.

From the perspective of the individual Jew, this conduct might seem hypocritical: he or she appears to be feigning a faith no longer held. Yet from the community's perspective, and indeed from the perspective of Judaism itself, the entire enterprise is very different and far more promising. First, the concept of *t'shuvah,* return, suggests that the mind and heart can be opened to Judaism at any time. Study, ritual practice, or synagogue attendance may lead to nothing, but they may also be a beginning. Moreover, like Jewish education, they are a response to the commandment to teach Judaism to one's children. One need not have perfect faith to conclude that children should learn Torah rather than skepticism. A parent's lack of faith may be replicated in the child, but it may not be—if the child is raised as a Jew with a religious identity.

And from the community's perspective, can the conclusion that only religion will guarantee its survival be *less* legitimate than the notion that only *ir*religion will do so? The Jewish leaders who have the courage to promote so radical a change in community behavior should not be cross-examined as to what is in their hearts, if the work of their hands holds promise for American Jewry. Whether their own personal motivation is love of God or an inherited sense of Jewish solidarity, they must know that only Judaism offers the American Jewish community a future.

It is said that Jews have made a "hedge" around the Torah to ensure that they do not even come close to violating its commandments. But it is also true that the Torah "has made a hedge around the Jews."[13] Unlike politics, the "hedge" of Torah does indeed separate Jews from their fellow citizens and bind them to each other.

Unlike ethnicity, it will not fade with the passage of time and generations. Unlike the "hedge" put around the Jewish people by their neighbors' anti-Semitism and unwillingness to marry Jews or to allow Jewish integration, the "hedge" of Torah does not depend on bigotry to function and will not fail when prejudice declines.

In the modern age, and especially in America, no one outside the Jewish community is building such a "hedge" to keep Jews in. If one is to exist, it must be generated by the Jews, and its only possible sustenance is their religious faith—their desire to be set apart at least in religious terms.

Yet these analyses fall short. They do explain what a Jew must do, and what the Jewish community must do, to work against the demographic disaster now facing the community. But they do not explain *why*. It can be proved with statistics that Judaism and Jewish schooling maintain Jewish identity and enable Jews to pass their faith on to their children. But all the statistics cannot answer the question, why does it matter? After all, today's intermarriage levels are a tribute to the openness and lack of prejudice in American society. If one does not resist or mourn, if indeed one celebrates, the mixing of Italian and Polish Americans, of Protestants and Catholics, of Japanese and Irish, why is the intermarriage of Jews alone a tragedy? What is the purpose of maintaining a separate Jewish community? What justifies endless efforts to resist the powerful currents of American society?

Rabbi Hayim Halevy Donin took up this point in his invaluable book, *To Be A Jew:*

> Let us face the issue squarely. Survival of Jewry is not in and of itself sufficient to justify loyalty to Judaism or on which to base the will to remain a Jew. If being a Jew has no meaning, then the survival of Jewry as a distinct people or faith is of no consequence.[14]

In each generation in America, those whose answer still lies in the tug of memory or some undefinable ethnic solidarity grow fewer and fewer, and external pressures to remain Jewish are now feeble indeed. The only answer capable of ensuring Jewish continuity in America lies in Judaism: in a religious faith that instructs the believer to remain a Jew, faithful to the covenant. For unless the community is based on faith in God, what possible purpose could there be for concern about its survival? Only Judaism can save the Jewish people, and, as Donin argues, only Judaism provides a justification for doing so.

What the Jewish sage Saadia Gaon said a thousand years ago in Babylonia remains true in America today: Jews are a people only by virtue of their Torah. They will decline if they are driven by fear of their neighbors, fear of their own traditions, and fear of the distinct identity that their covenant imposes on them as an article of faith. They will survive if they cling to their faith—to their Torah. It—and it alone—is for the Jews just what the Book of Proverbs calls it: a tree of life.

NOTES

Chapter 1. Crisis

1. Marshall Sklare, "Intermarriage and the Jewish Future," *Commentary* 37, no. 4 (April, 1964): 46.
2. Ibid., p. 52.
3. Thomas B. Morgan, "The Vanishing American Jew," *Look*, May 5, 1964.
4. Charles S. Liebman, *The Ambivalent American Jew* (Philadelphia, 1973), p. 193.
5. See Sergio della Pergola, "New Data on Demography and Identification Among Jews," in Paul Ritterband, ed., *Jewish Intermarriage in its Social Context* (New York, 1991), pp. 87–89; and Sidney Goldstein, "Profile of American Jewry: Insights from the 1990 National Jewish Population Survey," *American Jewish Yearbook*, 1992 (New York, 1992), pp. 126–27.
6. Charles E. Silberman, *A Certain People* (New York, 1985), p. 25.
7. Ibid., p. 274.
8. Ibid., p. 296.
9. Calvin Goldscheider, *Jewish Continuity and Change* (Bloomington, Ind., 1986), p. xiv.
10. Ibid., p. 152.
11. Ibid., p. 181.
12. Ibid., p. 11.
13. Sergio della Pergola, "The Jewish People Today: A Demographic View," *Congress Monthly* 59, no. 4 (May/June 1992): 20.
14. Paul Ritterband, "Only by Virtue of Its Torah," in Paul Ritterband, ed., *Jewish Intermarriage in Its Social Context* (New York, 1991), p. 99.

15. U. O. Schmelz and Sergio della Pergola, "Basic Trends in American Jewish Demography," in Steven Bayme, ed., *Facing the Future* (New York, 1989), p. 102.

16. Seymour Martin Lipset and Earl Raab, *Jews and the New American Scene* (Cambridge, Mass., 1995), p. 74.

17. Donald Feldstein, *The American Jewish Community in the 21st Century* (New York, 1984), p. 17.

18. Sergio della Pergola and Uziel O. Schmelz, "American Jewish Marriages: Transformation and Erosion," *Studies in Contemporary Judaism* 5 (1989): 212.

19. Nathan Glazer, "New Perspectives on American Jewish Sociology," *American Jewish Year Book,* 1987 (New York, 1987), p. 8 [quoting Sidney Goldstein].

20. Barry Kosmin and Seymour P. Lachman, *One Nation Under God* (New York, 1993), p. 66.

21. See, for example, Jonathan Rabinowitz, "The Paradoxical Effects of Jewish Community Size on Jewish Communal Behavior," *Contemporary Jewry* 10, no. 1 (1989): 9.

22. Gary A. Tobin and Gabriel Berger, *Synagogue Affiliation: Its Implications for the 1990s,* Cohen Center for Modern Jewish Studies, Brandeis University, Research Report #9 (September 1993), p. 25.

23. Chaim Waxman, "Whither American Jewry," *Society* (November/December 1990): 34.

24. Sidney Goldstein, "Profile of American Jewry: Insights from the 1990 National Jewish Population Study," in *American Jewish Year Book,* 1992, pp. 89–92.

25. Kosmin and Lachman, *One Nation Under God,* p. 121.

26. Peter Y. Medding, Gary A. Tobin, Sylvia Barack Fishman, and Mordechai Rimor, "Jewish Identity in Conversionary and Mixed Marriages," *Jewish Sociology Papers,* American Jewish Committee (New York, 1992), p.38.

Chapter 2. From Faith to Fear

1. Frederic Cople Jaher, *A Scapegoat in the New Wilderness* (Cambridge, Mass., 1994), p. 122.

2. Leonard Dinnerstein, *Anti-Semitism in America* (New York, 1994), p. 9.

3. Naomi W. Cohen, *Jews in Christian America* (New York, 1992), p. 28. Typically, Maryland's constitution held that "no other test or qualification ought to be required, on admission to any office of trust or profit, than such oath of support and fidelity to this State . . . and a declaration of a belief in the Christian religion." Maryland Constitution, November 11, 1776, Section XXXV (reprinted in Jacob Rader Marcus, ed., *The Jew in the American World* [Detroit, 1996], p. 96).

4. Melvin I. Urofsky, *American Zionism* (Lincoln, Neb., 1995), pp. 55–56.

5. Cohen, *Jews in Christian America,* p. 34.

6. Abraham Cahan, *The Rise of David Levinsky* (1960 edition), p. 110; quoted in Frieda Kerner Furman, *Beyond Yiddishkeit* (Albany, N.Y., 1987), p. 20.

7. The Rabbi of Slutsk, addressing a meeting of Orthodox Jews in New York City. See Sara Bershtel and Allen Graubard, *Saving Remnants* (Berkeley, Calif., 1992), p. 167.

8. Nathan Glazer, *American Judaism* (Chicago, 1957), pp. 133–34.

9. Quoted in Daniel J. Elazar, ed., *The New Jewish Politics* (Lanham, Md., 1988), pp. 10–11.

10. Egon Mayer, "Intermarriage, Outreach, and a New Agenda for Jewish Survival," *Journal of Jewish Communal Service* (Summer 1990): 202.

11. Cohen, *Jews in Christian America,* p. 40.

12. Jerold S. Auerbach, *Rabbis and Lawyers* (Bloomington, Ind., 1990).

13. Ibid., pp. xvi–xvii.

14. Ibid., p. 14.

15. See ibid., pp. 14, 17.

16. Ibid.

17. Urofsky, *American Zionism,* p.128.

18. Auerbach, *Rabbis and Lawyers,* p. 150.

19. Naomi W. Cohen, *Not Free to Desist* (Philadelphia, 1972), p. 434.

20. Cohen, *Jews in Christian America,* p. 126.

21. Bernard J. Bamberger, *The Synagogue Council of America: A Brief History* (New York, 1964), p. 81.

22. Cohen, *Jews in Christian America,* pp. 4–5, 240.

23. *Board of Education v. Mergens,* 496 U.S. 226 (1990).

24. Christopher Lasch, *Revolt of the Elites* (New York, 1995); quoted in Robert Bork, *Commentary* (February 1995): 28.

25. American Jewish Congress et al., amicus curiae brief on petition for a writ of certiorari to the New York State Court of Appeals, in *Board of Education of The Kiryas Joel Village School District,* Petitioner, v. *Louis Grumet and Albert V. Hawk,* Respondents, United States Supreme Court, October Term 1993, No. 93–517, 527, 539, at p. 62.

26. Quoted in David G. Dalin, ed., *From Marxism to Judaism: Collected Essays of Will Herberg* (Marcus Wiener, New York, 1989) p. 200.

27. Nathan Lewin, "The Church-State Game: A Symposium on Kiryas Joel," *First Things* 47 (November 1994): 39–40.

28. Nathan Lewin, "Note: The Free Exercise Boundaries of Permissible Accommodation Under the Establishment Clause," *Yale Law Journal* 99, no. 27 (1990): 1142–43. In the briefs to lower courts, the school superintendent was supported by every non-Orthodox Jewish group in saying that the state's establishment of the new school district "furthers the Hasidim's centrally held religious belief of insulating the children of the Village from the larger, diverse outside society" and "therefore has as its purpose, and/or will have as its primary effect, the promotion of religion."

29. *Capitol Square Review and Advisory Board v. Pinette* is No. 94–329; *Rosenberger v. Rector and Visitors of the University of Virginia* is No. 94–780.

30. Amicus curiae brief in *Rosenberger* by American Jewish Congress and Anti-Defamation League of B'nai B'rith, p. 4.

31. Amicus curiae brief in *Rosenberger* submitted by People for the American Way, the Baptist Joint Committee on Public Affairs, the National Council of Churches, the American Jewish Congress, the Union of American Hebrew Congregations, Hadassah, and the Womens' Zionist Organization of America, pp. 15, 24.

32. Quoted in Terry Eastland, ed., *Religious Liberty in the Supreme Court* (Washington, 1993), pp. 445–46.

33. Justice Scalia noted in his dissent that "maintaining respect for the religious observances of others is a fundamental civic virtue that government (including the public schools) can and should cultivate.." Id. at 460. Perhaps more strikingly, President Clinton shared this criticism of the decision, saying in 1995 "I didn't agree with that [decision] because I didn't think it any coercion at all. And I thought people were not interfered with. And I didn't think it amounted to the establishment of a religious practice by the government." President Clinton, "Remarks by the President on Religious Liberty in America," James Madison High School, Vienna, Va., July 12, 1995.

Chapter 3. The Gospel About Jews

1. Hillel Levine, "Evangelicals and Jews: Shared Nightmares and Common Cause," in A. James Rudin & Marvin Wilson, eds., *A Time To Speak* (Grand Rapids, Mich., 1997), p. 156.

2. Leon Klenicki, "Toward A Process of Healing: Understanding the Other as a Person of God," in Leon Klenicki, ed., *Toward A Theological Encounter* (Mahwah, N.J., 1991), pp. 1, 29.

3. Leonard Dinnerstein, *Anti-Semitism in America* (New York, 1994), p. 239.

4. Mordecai Waxman, "The Dialogue, Touching New Bases?" in Helga G. Croner, ed., *More Stepping Stones to Jewish-Christian Relations* (Mahwah, N.J., 1985), p. 28.

5. "Jewish Bigs Find Hurdles Remain After Pope Parley," *Forward,* October 13, 1995, p. 1.

6. These quotations, as well as those from the *Notes on the Correct Way to Present Jews and Judaism in Preaching and Catechesis in the Roman Catholic Church, the Guidelines for the Evaluation of Dramatizations of the Passion,* and *God's Mercy Endures Forever,* are provided in Philip A. Cunningham, *Education for Shalom* (Collegeville, Minn., 1995).

7. Quoted in Eugene J. Fisher & Leon Klenicki, eds., *In Our Time* (Mahwah, N.J., 1990), p. 86.

8. Cathechism of the Catholic Church (Dublin: 1994), para. 839, p. 195.

9. Quoted in *Pope John Paul II On Jews and Judaism, 1979–1986* (Washington, D.C., 1987), p. 82.

10. Quoted in Eugene J. Fisher, "'The Church and Racism': Implications for Catholic-Jewish Dialogue," in Eugene J. Fisher and Leon Klenicki, *Anti-Semitism Is a Sin* (New York, 1990), p. 3.

11. "Study Outline on the Mission and Witness of the Church," in Helga Croner, ed., *More Stepping Stones to Jewish-Christian Relations* (Mahwah, N.J., 1985), pp. 50–51.

12. Ibid., p. 52.

13. Eugene J. Fisher, "Update on Catholic Preaching and Teaching About Jews and Judaism," in *Christian Education and the Presentation of Judaism, In Dialogue,* vol. 2 (Washington, D.C., 1994), p. 51.

14. See Eugene J. Fisher, *Faith Without Prejudice* (New York, 1993), pp. 112–19.

15. Fisher, "Update on Catholic Preaching," p. 55.
16. Cunningham, *Education for Shalom,* p. 122.
17. Ibid., p. 100.
18. Ibid. pp. 104, 111, 112.
19. Quoted in Donald G. Dawe and Aurelia T. Fule, eds., *Christians and Jews Together* (Louisville, Ky., 1991), p. 9.
20. See, for example, *The Theology of the Churches and the Jewish People* (Geneva, 1988).
21. Ibid., pp. 61–62.
22. Harold Ditmanson, ed., *Stepping Stones to Further Jewish-Lutheran Relations* (Minneapolis, 1990), p. 62.
23. Ibid., p. 66.
24. Ibid., p. 69.
25. Ibid., p. 73.
26. Franklin Sherman, "Interfaith Focus: Luther, Lutheranism, and the Jews" (New York, 1995), p. 14.
27. "The Relationship Between United Church of Christ and the Jewish Community," *Minutes of the 16th General Synod of the United Church of Christ,* June, 1987, pp. 67–68.
28. "A Message to the Churches," Theological Panel on Jewish-Christian Relations, United Church of Christ (May 1990), p. 2.
29. Ibid.
30. "A Theological Understanding of the Relationship Between Christians and Jews," *Minutes of the 199th General Assembly, 1987,* Presbyterian Church (USA), vol. 1, p. 421. This document is also reprinted in Dawe and Fule, *Christians and Jews Together.*
31. Ibid., pp. 421–22.
32. Ibid., p. 420.
33. Ibid., pp. 420–21.
34. Ibid., p. 420.
35. "Report from the Commission on Theology: A Statement on Relations Between Jews And Christians," Christian Church/Disciples of Christ, 1993.
36. Stuart Polly, "The Portrayal of Jews and Judaism in Current Protestant Teaching Materials" (Ph.D. diss., Teachers' College, Columbia University, 1992).
37. Quoted in ibid., pp. 307–8.
38. Ibid., p. 311.

39. Ibid., p. 322.

40. Ibid., p. 325.

41. Stuart Polly, "What Are Protestants Teaching Their Teenagers About Jews and Judaism?" in *Christian Education and the Presentation of Judaism, In Dialogue* vol. 2 (New York, 1994), p. 25.

42. Quoted in Dawe and Fule, *Christians and Jews Together,* p. 14.

43. David Novak, "A Jewish Response," in Dawe and Fule, *Christians and Jews Together,* pp. 82, 90–91.

44. See the comment by Michael Wyschogrod, the former director of the Institute of Jewish-Christian Relations at the American Jewish Congress, "Jewish Survival in the Context of Jewish-Christian Dialogue," in Dawe and Fule, *Christians and Jews Together,* p. 120: "It is a lesson of history that a hard Christian line on the question of evangelization of Jews threatens Jewish well-being. If Jews are seen as doomed to hell as long as they persist in the nonacceptance of Jesus as Savior, the potential for the translation of this theological conviction into active persecution of Jews is very real."

45. "A Message to the Churches," Theological Panel on Jewish-Christian Relations, United Church of Christ (May, 1990), p. 3.

46. Ibid., p. 1.

47. "The American Lutheran Church and the Jewish Community," in Ditmanson, *Stepping Stones to Further Jewish-Lutheran Relations,* p. 74.

48. *A Theological Understanding of the Relationship Between Christians and Jews,* 199th General Assembly, Presbyterian Church (USA), pp. 8–9.

49. Mordecai Waxman, "The Dialogue, Touching New Bases?" in Helga G. Croner, ed., *More Stepping Stones to Jewish-Christian Relations,* p. 29.

Chapter 4. Evangelicals

1. Tom W. Smith, "Anti-Semitism in Contemporary America" (New York: American Jewish Committee, 1994), pp. 25–26.

2. Alan M. Dershowitz, *Chutzpah* (New York, 1991), p. 325.

3. Address of Alexander M. Schindler, Board of Trustees, Union of American Hebrew Congregations, November 22, 1980, quoted in David A. Rausch, *Communities in Conflict/Evangelicals and Jews* (Philadelphia, 1991), p. 158.

4. Quoted in Yehiel Eckstein, *What You Should Know About Jews and Judaism* (Waco, Tex., 1994), p. 318.

5. Rausch, *Communities in Conflict/Evangelicals and Jews,* p. 66.

6. Nathan Perlmutter, "Jews and Fundamentalists," *Reconstructionist,* December 1985, p. 20.

7. *The Religious Right: The Assault on Tolerance and Pluralism in America* (New York: Anti-Defamation League, 1994), p. 8.

8. Rausch, *Communities in Conflict/Evangelicals and Jews,* p. 66.

9. David A. Rausch, *Fundamentalist-Evangelicals and Anti-Semitism* (Valley Forge, Pa., 1993), p. 49.

10. See, e.g., the material discussed in Polly, "The Portrayal of Jews and Judaism," p. 355, and Stuart Polly, "What Are Protestants Teaching Their Teenagers About Jews and Judaism?" in *Christian Education and the Presentation of Judaism, In Dialogue,* vol. 2 (New York: Anti-Defamation League, 1994), p. 26.

11. Tom W. Smith, *What Do Americans Think About Jews* (New York, 1991), p. 22. This is contrary to earlier research results, as Smith notes: "Research from the 1960s . . . found that orthodox religious beliefs, being a fundamentalist, and religious particularism were associated with religious anti-Semitism, and, in turn, with secular anti-Semitism. . . . However, later reanalysis suggested that their model was inaccurate. Subsequent research has found only weak or qualified associations between religious factors and anti-Semitism. . . . At present, it does not appear that either fundamentalist religious beliefs or a higher commitment to Christianity are [sic] notably associated with anti-Semitism, although religion was arguably the major factor in its early development," (citations omitted), pp. 24–25.

12. *Highlights from an Anti-Defamation League Survey on Anti-Semitism and Prejudice in America* (New York: Anti-Defamation League, 1992), p. 34.

13. "Christian Right Defies Categories," *New York Times,* July 22, 1994, p. A1.

14. "Indicators," *The American Enterprise* (February, March, April 1995), p. 19.

15. Rausch, *Fundamentalist-Evangelicals,* p. 207.

16. "Robertson Gets Neo-Con Confidence Vote," *Forward,* March 17, 1995, p. 2.

17. Stephen Carter, *The Culture of Disbelief* (New York, 1993), pp. 228–29.

18. *The Religious Right: The Assault on Tolerance and Pluralism in America* (New York, 1994), p. 53.

19. Ibid., pp. iv, 41.

20. Letter from Abraham Foxman to Pat Robertson, August 3, 1994.
21. *The Religious Right*, p. 7.
22. Ibid., p. 53.
23. Ibid., p. 145.
24. Marvin R. Wilson, "An Evangelical Perspective on Judaism," in Marc H. Tanenbaum, Marvin R. Wilson, and A. James Rudin, eds., *Evangelicals and Jews in Conversation on Scripture, Theology, and History* (Grand Rapids, Mich., 1978), p. 18.
25. Quoted in Harold Ditmanson, ed., *Stepping Stones to Further Jewish-Lutheran Relations* (Minneapolis, 1990), pp. 77–78.
26. Ibid., p. 79.
27. Vernon C. Grounds, "The Problem of Proselytization," in Tanenbaum et al., *Evangelicals and Jews,* pp. 207–8.
28. Quoted in Rausch, *Communities in Conflict,* p. 28.
29. "Reform Leader Seeking An Evangelical Judaism," *Forward,* October 29, 1993, p. 1.
30. Yehiel Eckstein, *What You Should Know About Jews and Judaism* (Waco, Tex., 1994), p. 321.
31. "Study Outline on the Mission and Witness of the Church," in Helga Croner, ed., *More Stepping Stones to Jewish-Christian Relations* (Mahwah, N.J., [1985]), p. 52.
32. Quoted in Polly, "The Portrayal of Jews," p. 293.
33. Eckstein, *What You Should Know About Jews and Judaism,* pp. 297–98.
34. Ibid., p. 295.
35. Ibid., pp. 298–99.
36. Quoted in Polly, "The Portrayal of Jews," pp. 80–81.
37. Vernon C. Grounds, "The Problem of Proselytization," pp. 215–16.
38. Ibid., p. 220.
39. Quoted in Tanenbaum et al., *Evangelicals and Jews,* pp. 259–62.
40. Ibid., p. 263.
41. Remarks of Ralph E. Reed Jr. to the Anti-Defamation League of B'nai B'rith, April 3, 1995.
42. "Resolution on Anti-Semitism," Southern Baptist Convention, 1972, quoted in Helga Croner, ed., *Stepping Stones to Further Jewish-Christian Relations* (New York, 1977), p. 110.
43. Polly, "What Are Protestants Teaching Their Teenagers About Jews and Judaism?," p. 26.
44. Rausch, *Communities in Conflict,* p. 69.
45. Ibid., p. 69.

46. Ibid., p. 71.
47. Quoted in ibid., p. 72.
48. Ibid., p. 78.
49. Ibid., p. 82.
50. Paul Pierson, *Themes From Acts* (Ventura, Calif., 1982), pp. 29–30.
51. David A. Rausch, "What and How Evangelicals Teach about Jews and Judaism," in A. James Rudin and Marvin R. Wilson, *A Time to Speak* (Grand Rapids, Mich., 1987), p. 79.
52. Polly, *The Portrayal of Jews*, p. 128.
53. Quoted ibid., p. 127.
54. Quoted in ibid,. pp. 253–54. One could cite numerous other examples. The reference to believers and unbelievers today appears elsewhere as well. A book put out by Scripture Press, another major evangelical textbook supplier, teaches that "The Book of Hebrews was written to Jewish believers who needed to remember that Jesus is better than the laws of Judaism. Early believers needed such reminders, and so do we." (Quoted in Polly, *The Portrayal of Jews*, p. 236.) A Southern Baptist text says,

   "The old covenant, or the law, was rigid and was to be observed without question. . . . (This type of faith was practiced by Jews who rejected Christ even after Christ's resurrection.)" (Quoted in ibid., p. 249.)

55. Quoted in ibid., p. 218.
56. Quoted in ibid., p. 252.
57. See ibid., p. 360.
58. See the remark of Father Flannery, quoted in Polly, "What Are Protestants Teaching Their Teenagers About Jews and Judaism?," p. 167. ("[T]here is a certain boundary, often difficult to locate, across which Christian theological anti-Judaism is transformed into Christian anti-Semitism. In other words, the principal source of Christian anti-Semitism was the Church's anti-Judaism. It is apparent that there exists a certain level of theological negation or polemical intensity which, when reached, produces an effect that is no longer purely theological and has turned to hatred and stereotype—the life-blood of anti-Semitism.")
59. The July/August 1990 edition of Pat Robertson's Perspective, quoted in *The Religious Right* (Anti-Defamation League, New York, 1994), p. 13.
60. The September 1980 edition of *Pat Robertson's Perspective,* quoted in *The Religious Right*, p. 16.

61. The May/June 1989 edition of *Pat Robertson's Perspective,* quoted in *The Religious Right,* pp. 21–22.

62. Editorial, *Christianity Today,* April 24, 1981, p. 12.

63. Richard W. Riley, *Religious Expression in Public Schools* (U.S. Department of Education), August 10, 1995.

64. Quoted in Seymour Siegel, "The Meaning of Israel in Jewish Thought," in Tanenbaum et al., *Evangelicals and Jews,* p. 116.

65. Ibid., p. 112.

Chapter 5. Intermarriage

1. Lawrence Grossman, "Jewish Communal Affairs," *American Jewish Year Book* 1993 (New York, 1993), p. 179.

2. Ibid.

3. Kosmin and Lachman, *One Nation Under God* (New York, 1993), p. 240.

4. Yisrael Ellman, "Intermarriage in the United States: A Comparative Study of Jews and Other Ethnic and Religious Groups," *Jewish Social Studies* 49, no. 1 (1987): 4.

5. Betty Lee Sung, "Chinese American Intermarriage," *Journal of Comparative Family Studies* 21, no. 2 (Summer 1990): 351.

6. Richard D. Alba, *Italian Americans* (Englewood Cliffs, N.J., 1985), pp. 146-49, Table 5-1.

7. Richard D. Alba, "Assimilation's Quiet Tide, *Public Interest* No. 119 (Spring 1995): 14.

8. Richard D. Alba, *Italian Americans,* pp. 160–61.

9. Paul Spickard, *Mixed Blood* (Madison, Wis., 1989), p. 181.

10. Yisrael Ellman, "Intermarriage in the United States: A Comparative Study of Jews and Other Ethnic Groups," *Jewish Social Studies* 49, no. 1 (1987): 1.

11. Michel-Guillaume Jean de Crèvecoeur, *Letters From an American Farmer,* Letter #3.

12. Marshall Sklare, "Intermarriage and the Jewish Future," *Commentary* (April 1964): p. 52.

13. Jonathan D. Sarna, "Interreligious Marriage in America," in *The Intermarriage Crisis* (American Jewish Committee, New York, 1991), p. 2.

14. Steven M. Cohen, *Content or Continuity* (New York, 1991), p. 33 and Table 25.

15. Charlotte Holstein, "When Commitments Clash: One Leader's Personal Dilemma," in *The Intermarriage Crisis* (American Jewish Committee, New York, 1991), p. 36. This is one example of a broader phenomenon. Steven Bayme of the American Jewish Committee has noted that "All too often communal policy is guided by the emotional desires of Jewish leaders that their grandchildren remain Jews." Steven Bayme, "Enhancing Jewish Identity: Form and Content," address to the Wilstein Institute of Jewish Policy Studies, Council of Jewish Federations, University of Judaism, July 9, 1991. Bayme later wrote that "The rational approach to communal policy on any problem is often inhibited by the emotional needs of Jewish communal leaders. Frequently, policy discussion is colored by well-intentioned desires to provide human consolation to those affected. These, to be sure, are noble sentiments. They form, however, a disastrous base on which to formulate communal policy." Steven Bayme, "Intermarriage and Communal Policy: Prevention, Conversion, and Outreach," in Avis Miller, Janet Marder, and Steven Bayme, *Approaches to Intermarriage* (American Jewish Committee, New York, 1993), p. 9.

16. Egon Mayer, "Why Not Judaism," Moment, October 1991, quoted in Sylvia Barack Fishman and Alice Goldstein, "When They Are Grown They Will Not Depart," Cohen Center for Modern Jewish Studies, Brandeis University, Research Report 8 (March 1993), p. 17 n. 7.

17. Egon Mayer, "Intermarriage: Beyond the Gloom and Doom," *San Diego Jewish Press*, November 13, 1992, quoted in Ibid., p. 17, n. 8.

18. Egon Mayer, "Jewish Continuity in An Age of Intermarriage," in *Symposium on Intermarriage and Jewish Continuity*, vol. 1, Council of Jewish Federations General Assembly, Baltimore, Md., November 21, 1991.

19. Sylvia Barack Fishman, Mordechai Rimor, Gary A. Tobin, and Peter Y. Medding, *Intermarriage and American Jews Today; New Findings and Policy Implications* (Cohen Center, Brandeis University, October 1990), p. 20.

20. Jack Wertheimer, *A People Divided* (New York, 1993), p. 107.

21. Mark L. Winer, Sanford Seltzer, and Steven J. Schwager, *Leaders of Reform Judaism* (New York, 1987), p. 131.

22. Ibid., p. 141.

23. "Interfaith Couples Get to Visit Israel Thanks to the UJA," *Forward*, August 18, 1995, p. 1.

24. *Jewish Outreach Institute Newsletter*, vol. 1, No. 3, p. 6.

25. Grossman, "Jewish Communal Affairs," p. 179.

26. Alice Goldstein and Sylvia Barack Fishman, *Teach Your Children When*

They Are Young: Contemporary Jewish Education in the United States (Research Report #10, Cohen Center, Brandeis University, December 1993), p. 11.

27. Ibid., p. 12.
28. Peter Y. Medding, Gary A. Tobin, Sylvia Barack Fishman, and Mordechai Rimor, *Jewish Identity in Conversionary and Mixed Households* (Jewish Sociology Papers, American Jewish Committee, 1992), p. 37.
29. Steven M. Cohen, *Content or Continuity,* Table 33, p. 79.
30. Medding et al., *Jewish Identity,* p. 32.
31. Winer et al., *Leaders of Reform Judaism,* p. 42.
32. Cohen, *Content or Continuity,* Table 33, p. 79.
33. Stanley Lieberson and Mary C. Waters, *From Many Strands* (New York, 1988), p. 213.
34. Steven Bayme, "Changing Perceptions of Intermarriage," *Journal of Jewish Communal Service* (Summer 1990): 221.
35. Egon Mayer, *Children of Intermarriage* (New York: American Jewish Committee, 1989), p. 24, 29.
36. Alba, *Italian Americans,* pp. 154–155.
37. The term is used by Sergio della Pergola in "The Jewish People Today: A Demographic View," *Congress Monthly* 59, no. 4 (May/June 1992): 20.
38. Mayer, *Children of Intermarriage* (New York, 1989), p. 24.
39. Ibid., pp. 14–15, 45.
40. Jonathan Sarna, "Reform Jewish Leaders, Intermarriage, and Conversion," *CCAR Journal* (Winter 1990): 7.
41. Mayer, *Children of Intermarriage,* Table 27, p. 34.
42. Lydia Kukoff, "A Decade of Reform Jewish Outreach: Achievement and Promise," in Egon Mayer, ed., *Jewish Intermarriage, Conversion, and Outreach* (Center for Jewish Studies, The Graduate School and University Center, City University of New York, 1990), p. 50.
43. David W. Belin, "Confronting the Intermarriage Crisis with Realism and Effective Action," in *The Intermarriage Crisis* (American Jewish Committee, New York, 1991), p. 41.
44. Barry Kosmin, "The Demographic Imperatives of Outreach," *Journal of Jewish Communal Service* (Summer 1990): 210.
45. Seymour Martin Lipset and Earl Raab, *Jews and the New American Scene* (Cambridge, Mass., 1995), p. 68.
46. The study, Egon Mayer and Amy Avgar, *Conversion Among the Intermarried* (New York: American Jewish Committee, 1987), is mentioned in Egon Mayer, "Intermarriage Research at the American Jewish Committee: Its

Evolution and Impact," in Steven Bayme, ed., *Facing the Future* (New York, 1989), p. 175.

47. Egon Mayer, *Intermarriage and Rabbinic Officiation* (American Jewish Committee, New York, 1989), p. 8.

48. Mayer and Avgar, *Conversion Among the Intermarried,* p. 15.

49. Spickard, *Mixed Blood,* p. 195.

50. Mayer and Avgar, *Conversion Among the Intermarried,* p. 10.

51. Winer et al., *Leaders of Reform Judaism,* p. 90.

52. Jacob B. Ukeles, "Does Outreach Justify Investment—Alternatives to Outreach," in *The Intermarriage Crisis* (New York: William Petschek National Family Center, American Jewish Committee, New York, 1991), p. 19.

53. Diane Solomon, "Outreach, Inreach, and Overreach," *Moment* 20, no. 1 (February 1995): 54.

54. Michael A. Meyer, "On the Slope Toward Syncretism and Sectarianism," *CCAR Journal* (Summer 1993): 41.

55. Ibid., p. 42.

56. Ibid., p. 44.

57. Eugene Borowitz, *A New Jewish Theology in the Making* (Philadelphia, 1968), pp. 53–54.

58. Lawrence J. Epstein, "The Patrilineal Principle: A Time for Clarification," *CCAR Journal* (Summer 1992): 59.

59. "Reform Jews Oppose Training in 2 Religions," *Washington Times,* December 4, 1995, p. A5.

60. "Wanted: Rabbi Who Does Intermarriages," *Forward,* February 9, 1996, p. 2.

Chapter 6. The Flight from Judaism

1. Nathan Glazer, *American Judaism* (Chicago, 1957), p. 132.

2. George Gallup Jr. and Joseph Castelli, *The People's Religion: American Faith in the 90s* (New York, 1989), p. 116.

3. Quoted in Barry A. Kosmin and Seymour P. Lachman, *One Nation Under God* (New York, 1993), p. 76.

4. Renae Cohen and Sherry Rosen, *Organizational Affiliation of American Jews: A Research Report* (New York, 1992), pp. 8, 25–26.

5. Steven M. Cohen, *Content or Continuity* (New York, 1991), pp. 64–69.

6. Mark Winer, Sanford Seltzer, and Steven J. Schwager, *Leaders of Reform Judaism* (New York, 1987), p. 50.

7. *Los Angeles Times,* "Israel and the Palestinian Problem," study no. 149, fieldwork March 29 to April 17, 1988.

8. Jack Wertheimer, *A People Divided* (New York, 1993), p. 51.

9. "Most Americans Say Religion Is Important to Them," *The Gallup Poll Monthly,* February 1995, pp. 18–19.

10. Glazer, *American Judaism,* p. 91.

11. Jonathan Woocher, *Sacred Survival: The Civil Religion of American Jews* (Bloomington, Ind., 1986), pp. vii, 24.

12. Melvin I. Urofsky, *American Zionism* (Lincoln, Neb., 1995), p. 75.

13. Woocher, *Sacred Survival,* pp. 85–86.

14. Ibid., p. 32.

15. Ibid., p. 52.

16. "As Peace Beckons, Hadassah Feels Its Age," *Forward,* July 29, 1994, p. 1.

17. "B'nai B'rith Race Marred by 'Deceit,'" *Forward,* August 19, 1994, p. 1.

18. Herbert A. Friedman, "UJA—Exploring New Paths," *Moment,* December 1991, p. 25.

19. Gary A. Tobin, "A Profile of Major Donors' Attitudes and Behavior Towards Jewish Philanthropic Giving," Cohen Center for Modern Jewish Studies, Brandeis University, Policy and Planning Paper #7 (March 1992), p. 8.

20. Gary A. Tobin, "Trends in American Jewish Philanthropy: Market Research Analysis," Cohen Center for Modern Jewish Studies, Brandeis University (April 1992), p. 22. See also "Threat to Federation System Seen by New Harvard Study," *Forward,* January 19, 1996, p. 8.

21. Gary A. Tobin, "Israel and the Changing Character of Fundraising," Cohen Center for Modern Jewish Studies, Brandeis University, Research Report #11 (April 1994), p. 5.

22. Gary A. Tobin, "Trends in American Jewish Philanthropy," p. 14.

23. Woocher, *Sacred Survival,* p. 92.

24. See text accompanying Chapter 3, notes 21–22.

25. See Deborah Lipstadt, "From Noblesse Oblige to Personal Redemption: the Changing Profile and Agenda of American Jewish Leaders," *Modern Judaism* 4 (October 1984): 304–5.

26. Daniel J. Elazar, "Developments in Jewish Continuity: Organization in the Second Postwar Generation," in Seymour Martin Lipset, ed., *American Pluralism and the Jewish Community* (New Brunswick, N.J., 1990), pp. 177–78.

27. Steven Bayme, "Enhancing Jewish Identity: Form and Content," Address to the Wilstein Institute of Jewish Policy Studies, Council of Jewish Federations, University of Judaism (July 9, 1991).

28. Wertheimer, *A People Divided,* p. xiv.

29. Charles S. Liebman and Steven M. Cohen, *Two Worlds of Judaism* (New Haven, 1990), p. 84.

30. See the discussion in Urofsky, *American Zionism,* pp. 33–43.

31. Ibid., p. 33.

32. David Dalin, *From Marxism to Judaism: Collected Essays of Will Herberg* (New York: Marcus Wiener Publishing, 1989), p. 118.

33. Urofsky, *American Zionism,* p. 95.

34. David A. Rausch, *Fundamentalist-Evangelicals and Anti-Semitism* (Valley Forge, Pa., 1993), p. 34.

35. Quoted in Michael A. Meyer, "A Centennial History," in Samuel E. Karff, ed., *Hebrew Union College—Jewish Institute of Religion At One Hundred Years* (Cincinnati: Hebrew Union College Press, 1976), p. 45.

36. Ibid.

37. Urofsky, *American Zionism,* p. 128.

38. Melvin I. Urofsky, "Zionism and American Politics," in Robert M. Seltzer and Norman J. Cohen, eds., *The Americanization of the Jews* (New York, 1995), p. 156.

39. Leonard Fein, *Where Are We?* (New York, 1988), pp. 19, 82.

40. See Daniel J. Elazar, "The Jewish Context of the New Jewish Politics, in Daniel J. Elazar, ed., *The New Jewish Politics* (Lanham, Md., 1988), p. 75 (predicting that sometime after the year 2000, perhaps around 2010, Israel will become the largest Jewish community in the world, and that Hebrew will become the lingua franca of world Jewish activity); and Sergio della Pergola, "The Jewish People Today: A Demographic View," *Congress Monthly* 59, no. 4 (May/June 1992), p. 21 (predicting that, given higher birth rates in Israel than in the Diaspora, there will be more Jews living in Israel than in the Diaspora in the second quarter of the next century; if there is much emigration to Israel, this could come as soon as 2020).

41. The figure that emerged from the National Jewish Population Survey was 26.2 percent. See Sidney Goldstein, in "Profile of American Jewry: Insights from the 1990 National Jewish Population Survey," *American Jewish Year Book* 1992 (New York: American Jewish Committee, 1992), Table 23, p. 172. A survey conducted for the American Jewish Committee in 1995 estimated the figure at 37 percent. See *AJC Journal,* November 1995, p. 3.

42. Cohen, *Content or Continuity,* pp. 33, 34, 72 (Table 26).
43. Gary Tobin, "Israel and the Changing Character of Fundraising," Cohen Center for Modern Jewish Studies, Brandeis University, Research Report #11 (April 1994), p. 1.
44. "Jewish Charities Turn to Priorities at Home, " Forward, March 25, 1994, p. 1.
45. Steven Bayme, "Enhancing Jewish Identity: Form and Content," Address to the Wilstein Institute of Jewish Policy Studies, Council of Jewish Federations, University of Judaism (July 9, 1991).
46. Steven Cohen, *American Modernity and Jewish Identity* (New York, 1983), p. 163.
47. Charles S. Liebman, *Deceptive Images* (New Brunswick, N.J., 1988), pp. 86–87.
48. Whether Jewish liberalism has declined recently is now the subject of debate. See Earl Raab, "Are American Jews Still Liberal?," *Commentary 101,* No. 2 (February 1996): 43; Ed Miller, "Why the Jewish GOP Vote May Be Bigger Than You Think," *Washington Times,* November 28, 1995; and Joel Kotkin, "Questioning the Old-Time Religion," *New Democrat,* November/December 1995, p. 23.
49. See the analysis in Jerold S. Auerbach, *Rabbis and Lawyers* (Bloomington, Ind., 1990), p. 82.
50. Cohen, *American Modernity and Jewish Identity,* p. 155.
51. Ira Silverman, *American Jewish Year Book* 1991, p. 190.
52. Daniel J. Elazar, *Community and Polity* (Philadelphia, 1976), p. 274.
53. Quoted in Charles S. Liebman and Steven M. Cohen, *Two Worlds of Judaism,* p. 111.
54. Cohen, *American Modernity and Jewish Identity,* p. 35.
55. Marshall Sklare, *Jewish Identity on the Suburban Frontier* (Chicago, 1979), pp. 323–24.
56. Cohen, *American Modernity and Jewish Identity,* p. 32.
57. Winer et al., *Leaders of Reform Judaism,* p. 50.
58. Frieda Kerner Furman, *Beyond Yiddishkeit* (Albany, 1987), pp. 43, 64.
59. Lawrence Grossman, "Jewish Communal Affairs," *American Jewish Year Book 1991* (New York, 1991), p. 191.
60. Murray Friedman, *The Utopian Dilemma* (Washington, D.C., 1985), p. 84.
61. *Los Angeles Times,* "Israel and the Palestinian Problem, " study no. 149, fieldwork March 26 to April 17, 1988.
62. See Jack Wertheimer, "A Jewish Contract With America," *Commentary,* May 1995, p. 32.

63. Quoted in Edward S. Shapiro, *A Time for Healing: American Jewry Since World War II* (Baltimore, 1992), p. 227.

64. Michael Lerner, *Jewish Renewal: A Path to Healing and Transformation* (New York: 1994), pp. 336, 351, 359, 366.

65. Auerbach, *Rabbis and Lawyers,* pp. 24, 44–45.

66. Ibid., p. 60.

67. Ibid., p. 75.

68. Ibid., p. 66–67.

69. Address by Ted Lapkin, Des Moines, executive director of the Iowa Jewish Community Relations Council, to the Minkoff Institute Seminar, New York City, June 13, 1995.

70. Cohen, *Content or Continuity,* Table 14, p. 65.

71. Jacob Neusner, *Introduction to American Judaism* (Minneapolis, 1994), p. 117.

72. Jacob Neusner, *Stranger at Home* (Chicago, 1981), p. 81.

73. Michael Wyschograd, "Faith and the Holocaust," *Judaism* 20 (Summer 1971): quoted in Neusner, *Stranger at Home,* p. 77.

74. Cohen, *Content or Continuity,* Table 20, p. 69.

75. Steven M. Cohen, *The Dimensions of American Jewish Liberalism* (New York, American Jewish Committee, 1989), Table 1.3.

76. Liebman and Cohen, *Two Worlds of Judaism,* p. 44.

77. Quoted in Sara Bershtel and Allen Graubard, *Saving Remnants: Feeling Jewish in America* (Berkeley, 1993), p. 70.

78. Shapiro, *A Time for Healing: American Jewry Since World War II* (Baltimore, 1992), pp. 51–52.

79. Seymour Martin Lipset & Earl Raab, *Jews and the New American Scene* (Cambridge, Mass., 1995), p. 86.

80. Ibid., p. 87.

81. Tom. W. Smith, *Anti-Semitism in Contemporary America* (New York, 1994), p. 32.

82. Leonard Dinnerstein, *Anti-Semitism In America* (New York, 1994), pp. 243, 250.

83. Anti-Defamation League, *Highlights from an Anti-Defamation League Survey on Anti-Semitism and Prejudice in America* (New York, 1992), p. 30; see also Smith, *Anti-Semitism in Contemporary America,* pp. 27–28.

84. Tom W. Smith, *What Do Americans Think About Jews?* (New York: Anti-Defamation League, 1991), p. 27.

85. *Armed and Dangerous* (New York: Anti-Defamation League, 1994), p. 3.

86. *Militias: A Growing Danger* (New York: American Jewish Committee, 1995), p. 3.

87. Quoted in the *Washington Post,* March 3, 1996, p. C3.

88. Quoted in *The Neoconservative Imagination,* De Muth and Kristol, eds. (Washington, D.C., 1995), p. 203.

89. Arthur Hertzberg, *The Jews in America* (New York, 1989), p. 387.

Chapter 7. The Orthodox Nuisance

1. Charles S. Liebman, *Deceptive Images* (New Brunswick, N.J., 1988), pp. 50–51.

2. Jack Wertheimer, *A People Divided* (New York, 1993), p. 188.

3. David Landau, *Piety and Power* (London, 1993), pp. 24–25.

4. Hillel Levine and Lawrence Harmon, *The Death of an American Jewish Community* (New York, 1992), p. 7.

5. Ibid., p. 244.

6. Ibid., p. 259.

7. "When Jewish Leadership Was Tested Under Stress," *Forward,* November 18, 1994, p. 1.

8. "Jewish Heavies Backing Dinkins As Grass Roots Go for Giuliani," *Forward,* October 8, 1993, p. 1.

9. "Baby Boom Hits Jewish Day Schools As Yuppies Seek Yiddishkeit," *Forward,* July 21, 1995, p. 1.

10. Barry A. Kosmin and Seymour P. Lachman, *One Nation Under God* (New York, 1993), p. 271.

11. Barry A. Kosmin and Seymour P. Lachman, *One Nation Under God* (New York, 1993), p. 271. Donald Feldstein's study for the American Jewish Congress, *The American Jewish Community in the 21st Century,* reached almost the same conclusion.

12. "Vouchers Split Coast Jews," *Forward,* October 29, 1993, p. 1.

13. Sylvia Barack Fishman and Alice Goldstein, "When They Are Grown They Will Not Depart: Jewish Education and the Jewish Behavior of American Adults," Cohen Center for Modern Jewish Studies, *Research Report #8* (March, 1993), p. 2.

14. Ibid., p. 12.

15. "Jewish Involvement of the Baby Boom Generation," Mordechai Rimor and Elihu Katz, Louis Guttman Israel Institute of Applied Social Research Publication No. MR/1185B (Jerusalem, 1993), pp. 5, 9, 10.

16. John C. Convey, *Catholic Schools Make a Difference* (Washington, D.C.: National Catholic Educational Association, 1992), p. 38.

17. "Baby Boom Hits Jewish Day Schools," p. 1.

18. Michael J. Guerra, *Lighting New Fires: Catholic Schooling in America 25 Years After Vatican II* (Washington, D.C.: National Catholic Education Association, 1991), pp. 57; U.S. Department of Education, National Center for Education Statistics, *Digest of Education Statistics 1994* (Washington, D.C., 1994), pp.70–71; "Enrollment in Catholic Schools Up for Third Straight Year," *Education Week* 14, no. 31 (April 26, 1995): 7; "On The Road to Continuity, the Middle Class Is Left Behind," *Forward,* January 13, 1995, p. 1.

19. "How the Other Side Copes," *Forward,* January 13, 1995, p. 3.

20. Kosmin and Lachman, *One Nation Under God,* p. 271.

21. Michael J. Guerra, *Lighting New Fires: Catholic Schooling in America 25 Years After Vatican II* (Washington, D.C., 1991), p. 6.

22. Diane Ravitch, "Somebody's Children: Necessary Steps for Expanding Educational Opportunity," paper prepared for conference at Princeton University, May 24–26, 1994.

23. Rabbi Alan Silverstein [president of the Rabbinical Assembly], "Some Hard Questions We Should Be Asking Ralph Reed," *Metro West Jewish News,* December 7, 1995, p. 5.

24. Robert H. Bork, "What to Do About the First Amendment," *Commentary* 99, no. 2 (February 1995): 23.

25. Naomi Cohen, *Not Free to Desist* (Philadelphia, 1972), p. 435.

26. Charles S. Liebman, *Deceptive Images* (New Brunswick, N.J., 1988), p. 50

27. Leonard Fein, *Where Are We?* (New York, 1988), p. 41.

28. Steven M. Cohen, *Content or Continuity* (New York: American Jewish Committee, 1991), table 23, p. 71.

29. Jonathan Sacks, *One People: Tradition, Modernity, and Jewish Unity* (London, 1993), p. 39.

Chapter 8. Return

1. Will Herberg, "Anti-Semitism Today," *Commonweal,* July 16, 1954, reprinted in David Dalin, ed., *From Marxism to Judaism: Collected Essays of Will Herberg* (New York, 1989), p. 176.

2. Lucy Dawidowicz, *What Is the Use of Jewish History?* (New York, 1992), p. 263.

3. Jonathan Sacks, "Only Orthodox Judaism Will Enable the Jewish People to Survive," *Moment* (April 1992): 42.

4. Dennis Prager, "Why Do Jews Oppose School Prayer?" *Ultimate Issues* 10, no. 2 (1994): 7.

5. President Clinton, "Remarks by the President on Religious Liberty in America," James Madison High School, Vienna, Va., July 12, 1995.

6. Quoted in Robert H. Bork, "What to Do About the First Amendment," *Commentary* 99, no. 2 (February, 1995): 28.

7. Data cited in Gertrude Himmelfarb, *The De-Moralization of Society* (New York, 1995), pp. 223–27.

8. See the source materials cited in *Heritage Backgrounder 1064*, "Why Religion Matters: The Impact of Religious Practice on Social Stability" (Washington, D.C., 1996).

9. Steven Cohen, *American Modernity and Jewish Identity* (New York, 1983), p. 63.

10. Seymour Siegel, "Church and State," *Conservative Judaism* 18, nos. 3–4 (Spring/Summer, 1963): 7–8.

11. Ibid., p. 11.

12. Norman Podhoretz, *Making It* (New York, 1967), p. 26.

13. Paul Ritterband, "Only by Virtue of Its Torah," in Paul Ritterband, ed., *Jewish Intermarriage in Its Social Context* (Jewish Outreach Institute and Center for Jewish Studies, Graduate School of the City University of New York, 1991), p.100.

14. Hayim Halevy Donin, *To Be a Jew* (New York, 1972), p. 315.

INDEX